Divine Vegan Desserts

For Doris Fabry,
who never let a guest go unfed.

Thanks for everything, Mum.

Divine Vegan Desserts

Lisa Fabry

Grub Street • London

Published in 2012 by
Grub Street
4 Rainham Close
London SW11 6SS

Email: food@grubstreet.co.uk
Website: www.grubstreet.co.uk
Twitter @grub_street

Text copyright © Lisa Fabry, 2012
Copyright this edition © Grub Street, 2012
Edited by Julia Beaven, Wakefield Press
Designed by Liz Nicholson, designBITE
Typeset by Clinton Ellicott, Wakefield Press
Photographs by Heidi Linehan, www.heidiwho.com
Additional photographs by Esme Fabry

First published in Australia by Wakefield Press

A CIP catalogue for this book is available from the British Library
ISBN 978-1-908117-29-8

Printed and bound in Slovenia

contents

divine desserts

what's good about dessert?

Desserts have a bad reputation. They are seen to be bad for your teeth, your heart and your waistline. No wonder, when most desserts are made from white processed carbohydrates, saturated fat and refined sugar.

But there is another side to the story. Desserts can give you energy and lift your spirits. They look beautiful and deliver the pleasure of anticipation as well as the satisfaction of consumption. As for the unhealthy ingredients – refined sugar, white starches and saturated fat – these can be replaced with natural sweeteners or unrefined sugars, wholegrains and healthier vegetable milks, creams and oils. Other nutritious ingredients can be used in a dessert to supply nutrients that may have been lacking in the first course. For example, many children will often accept ingredients in dessert that they wouldn't dream of eating otherwise, such as carrot, pumpkin or sweet potato, ground nuts and seeds, or dried fruit purees. Some desserts can even be regarded as health foods, especially if they are raw or contain wholegrains, fruit or nuts.

guilty eating

You know what it feels like when someone starts an argument over dinner. Suddenly, your enthusiasm for eating disappears. Your throat constricts, your hunger is replaced by butterflies or nausea. If you continue to force yourself to eat, it feels like you are trying to digest a stone. It is clear that your digestive processes are affected by your emotions.

If you feel guilty when you eat dessert, what effect is this likely to have on your body? Traditional systems of medicine such as Ayurveda and Traditional Chinese Medicine have long accepted that emotions have a powerful influence on digestive and general health and these ideas are now becoming more commonplace in Western medicine. Feelings of shame and guilt have been linked with eating disorders and obesity and it has been suggested that emotional stress is the number one cause of digestive problems.

joyful eating

Let's think of food another way. You decide to make a cake. You take the time to find a recipe and read through the ingredients. You might replace white flour with wholemeal flour and white sugar with unrefined sugar. Perhaps you decide to add chopped walnuts, sesame seeds, and a handful of raisins. You are developing a healthy relationship with your food – and you haven't even started cooking.

Now it's time to bake. Like any creative activity – painting, writing, singing, gardening – baking connects what you *do* with what you *feel*. It can be an activity of inspiration and joy, if you are fully and mindfully engaged with the process. It can be a way of pouring your love – for yourself, your family, your friends – into what you are doing, so that love becomes embodied in the final product. How could eating something made from such carefully chosen ingredients and baked with such loving care be anything less than a divine experience?

We all need to eat. We need food to stay alive and be productive. I believe that we can combine this physical need with a spiritual sensibility by cultivating a connection with our food that reflects:

- a compassionate understanding of the environmental issues associated with food
- loving respect for our bodies and our health
- the expression of love, nurture and community through the creation and sharing of food
- a deep appreciation of the aesthetic qualities of food (colour, shape, aroma, texture, flavour) and its effects on our minds and bodies.

you are what you eat – listening to your body

If you go to a yoga class the teacher is likely to tell you, 'Listen to your body'. Meaning: 'Don't just *mindlessly* do what I tell you, even if it hurts like hell, be *mindfully* aware of your body.'

This is wise advice whatever you do with your body. Walking, gardening, dancing, making love – in each of these endeavours you will be more successful, enjoy yourself more and avoid pain and injury if you mindfully watch for cues from your body that tell you to act more, less or differently.

So it is with eating. It might seem obvious to exclude a food from your diet if you really dislike it or it makes you ill, but the time between cause and effect may be great, so it is not always clear what it is in your diet that is causing your migraines, digestive disorders, mood swings, weight gain, fungal infections, tiredness or allergies. Continuing to eat foods that are causing your body distress could lead to even more serious consequences: irritable bowel syndrome (IBS), high blood pressure, diabetes, heart disease or cancer.

But the good news is that you can learn to listen to your body. You can tune into its signals before they become too serious, and respond to them with a loving concern for your own wellbeing. And the more you do this, the easier it becomes, because as you reduce the load you place on your body it will become more finely tuned, more responsive. You can then notice your body's reaction to different foods and respond readily.

vegan desserts

I have been a vegetarian since my late teens, making that choice on ethical, moral, health and environmental grounds. Since then I never doubted my decision not to consume the dead flesh of another being.

In my thirties I developed symptoms of severe IBS and, after a long, difficult struggle to find some answers, finally decided to eliminate dairy from my diet. Almost overnight my pain was alleviated. A few weeks later I gave up eggs as well and felt even better.

As a vegan, my health improved rapidly, my IBS symptoms disappeared – and so did my constant sneezing and runny nose, what I thought were colds in winter and hay fever in summer. I had more energy, it was easier to keep my weight down and I was rarely sick. This was what it felt like to be healthy!

A vegan diet is healthier. The China Study, one of the biggest studies of nutrition ever undertaken (*The China Study*, Campbell and Campbell published by Wakefield Press), revealed that a diet that avoids meat, fish and dairy products is the healthiest; it promotes longevity and reduces disease. A vegan diet contains no dietary cholesterol, thus significantly reducing your risk of cardiovascular disease. Vegans tend to eat a diet high in wholegrains, fresh vegetables and fruit. This helps prevent macular degeneration, cataracts and high blood pressure. Vegans suffer less from arthritis, osteoporosis and type 2 diabetes. A plant-based diet is often recommended as part of the holistic management of many types of cancer. And by avoiding meat, you also avoid all the antibiotics, hormones and other chemicals ingested by the animals, eliminating your risk of catching animal-borne diseases, such as e-coli, salmonella or BSE.

A vegan diet is more compassionate and truly cruelty free. Billions of animals are killed each year for meat. The vegan and vegetarian website Happy Cow features a shocking real-time update on the exact numbers of animals that have died since you logged on (www.happycow.net/why_vegetarian.html). Millions of cows also suffer and die each year as a direct result of the dairy industry. To keep a cow producing milk, she must give birth regularly – these babies are taken away at birth and the males are killed for meat (www.milkmyths.org.uk). Far from the idealistic image of contented cows munching grass in a pasture or little lambs frolicking in the fields, animals in both the meat and dairy industry are often kept in overcrowded conditions, deprived of space, sunlight, veterinary care, access to the outdoors or contact with their mates or young. Animals, like us, are sensitive, intelligent creatures with emotions and feelings and treating them this way is inhumane.

A vegan diet is also better for the environment. On the most fundamental level, it simply takes fewer resources to grow vegetables than to raise animals. Plus, the production of meat is responsible for some of our worst environmental problems: polluted water systems, soil erosion, over-intensive farming and

overgrazing. Avoiding meat and dairy is one of the most effective ways of reducing greenhouse gas emissions. By switching from a meat-eating diet to a vegan diet, you save around two tons of CO_2 per person each year. Animal agriculture is responsible for the production of more than 100 million tons of methane a year (www.earthsave.org/globalwarming). Reducing meat consumption would have a significant effect on lowering methane levels in the atmosphere.

Veganism makes sense to me. Of course you would only want to put foods into your body that do not harm you, that lead you on a path towards optimum health, foods created without harming other creatures, for how can simply liking the taste of something override compassion when making food choices? And foods that are grown without harming the Earth, our precious home.

divine desserts around the world

One of the unique features of this book is the inclusion of a selection of divine vegan desserts being created around the world in cafes, restaurants and cooking classes. I have been lucky enough to visit some of the most talented vegan and vegetarian chefs in the world and taste some of the best vegan food on offer.

The food in every place I visited was created with a passion both for good eating and good health, reflecting a trend towards a more integrated approach to diet. The priority for a high quality, sensuous eating experience remains, but this is merged with a consciousness of how ingredients are produced, compassion for animals and the planet, and an awareness of the effect of what we eat on our total wellbeing.

I asked chefs from Australia, New Zealand, the west coast of the USA, and Europe to share their recipes so you can see that the creation of top-quality vegan desserts is not confined to the stainless-steel enclaves of international chefs, but can happen in your kitchen. This is by no means a comprehensive survey of vegan and vegetarian eating establishments. I'd love to include more next time, so please send your recommendations to lisa@divinevegan.com.

the quality of food

If you believe, as I do, that your health and wellbeing are dependent on the food you eat and your relationship to it, then good food should not be a luxury but a priority.

By good food I mean beautiful, inspiring food straight from nature. Food that comes off trees or out of the ground. Food as close to its original state as possible, uncontaminated by pesticides. Fresh fruits, vegetables, herbs, spices, beans, nuts, seeds, wholegrains, cold-pressed, unrefined oils and natural sweeteners. If the majority of your diet consists of these foods, you will be supporting your body to become optimally healthy.

When I buy food, I look for good quality produce that is:

- seasonal
- local
- organic
- fairtrade

Seasonal food is fresh. It hasn't been picked green, stored for months and then artificially gas-ripened. Eating seasonally means eating lighter foods such as melon and cucumber in summer; more warming foods such as pumpkins and potatoes in autumn. Seasonal food tastes better because natural ripening allows the flavours in the food to develop.

Local food is grown in your region. Buying local produce supports your local economy, even more so if you choose to shop at farmers' markets and food co-ops instead of supermarkets. It also significantly reduces food miles, the number of miles food has to travel from where it is produced to where it is consumed. This reduces your carbon footprint.

Organic food is grown without the aid of artificial fertilisers, pesticides and herbicides or genetically modified organisms (GMOs). Soil fertility is managed naturally and the long-term sustainability of the land is a high priority. It has been found that pesticides and herbicides from conventionally grown food can cause long-term health problems. Organic food is also more nutritious – recent studies in Europe show that organic food has higher levels of vitamins and antioxidants than conventionally grown food.

Fairtrade is an internationally agreed standard that aims to create a fairer international trading system. Small-scale farmers are often marginalised and disempowered by big business. Fairtrade helps them to have more of a say in the trade of their produce. Farmers and workers benefit because they are guaranteed longer-term trade relationships and fair prices. They receive technical training, help with business development and better health care and education. Fairtrade standards also help the environment by encouraging sustainable agricultural practices such as organic farming.

key ingredients in vegan baking

non-dairy milks

Cows' milk is for baby cows. It isn't intended for humans and there is a wealth of research to show that, contrary to popular belief, it is not a wholesome nutrient but actually detrimental to our good health. (*The Milk Imperative* by Russell Eaton is a good starting point.)

While we have all grown up being told that dairy products are essential to the development of healthy teeth and bones, this is not the case. It is easier for our bodies to obtain the calcium we need from broccoli, dark leafy greens, nuts, seeds and soy beans. A study in 2001 found that high animal protein intake may actually lead to increased bone loss and a higher risk of fractures (*A high ratio of dietary animal to vegetable protein increases the rate of bone loss and the risk of fracture in postmenopausal women*, Sellmeyer et al. American Journal of Clinical Nutrition 2001). To promote good bone health and prevent osteoporosis you need a balanced intake of protein, calcium, potassium and sodium, all available in a vegan diet.

There are many options for replacing cows' milk. Soy milk is the most commonly used substitute because it replaces the protein and fat found in dairy milk and provides the associated creaminess. Use a really good brand of soy milk for your dessert baking; one with creaminess but not the intrusive beany flavour. Look for a brand that doesn't contain added sweeteners or oil. And try to get one made from organic soy beans that have not been genetically modified.

Rice or oat milks work well in most recipes and are also widely available. Coconut milk can be used but has a characteristic flavour, which works in some dishes but not others.

You can also quite easily make your own nut and seed milks. Almost any kind of nut or seed can be used. Try almonds, brazils, cashews, hazelnuts, sunflower seeds or pumpkin seeds.

Make your own nut or seed milks

1. Take 1 cup any nut or seeds and soak overnight in filtered water.
2. Drain the water and place nuts or seeds in a blender.
3. Add 3 cups filtered water and blend until the nuts or seeds are as fine as possible.
4. Place a large piece of cheesecloth or muslin in a sieve over a large bowl.
5. Pour the blended mixture into the cloth-lined sieve and allow most of the liquid to drain through.
6. Here is the fun part! Wash your hands thoroughly or get food preparation gloves, and wear an apron. Gather up the edges of the cloth, twist the top and squeeze the bag with your hands to extract the rest of the liquid. Keep squeezing until all you have left is a bag of dryish nut fibre. You can use this as an addition to stews, pie fillings, cake mixtures or raw biscuits. Store it in the fridge.
7. If you wish to sweeten the milk, add vanilla, a little stevia or agave.
8. Bottle and store in the fridge. Use as fresh milk.

egg replacers

Eggs fulfil a variety of functions in baking so the replacer you choose will depend on the job it needs to do.

- Raising: baking powder, or a bicarbonate of soda/vinegar combination work extremely well, and I use one or both in most of my cakes.
- Binding and adding moisture: use apple sauce, sweet potato or pumpkin puree. Silken tofu and soy yogurt are good for adding moisture without a strong flavour. Ground flax seed and water makes a gooey slop which is an excellent binder. Proprietary brands of egg replacer, such as No-Egg in Australia and Europe or Ener-G in the USA, work well to bind ingredients but don't add much nutritional value to a recipe.
- Increasing the protein content of a dish, as well as binding: use soy or chickpea (besan) flour.

sugar and other sweeteners

Sugar is, as everyone knows, a delicious, but unnecessary addition to our diet. It is bad for our teeth, plays havoc with our blood sugar levels and has been linked to a variety of more serious health conditions such as mental health problems, gallstones and diabetes. The per capita consumption of refined sugar in the UK and Europe is between 30-40kg each year – that's almost 100g per person *every* day.

The World Health Association recommends we eat no more than 48 g (12 teaspoons) a day. The American Heart Association would like it to be closer to 25 g (6 teaspoons) for women and 38 g (9 teaspoons) for men. Based on these guidelines, I have marked as 'low sugar' any dessert which contains less than 12 g (3 teaspoons) refined sugar per serving, which is still half of the lowest of these recommendations. Most of the other recipes use less sugar than their conventional equivalents. You can work out the sugar content by dividing the total grams of sugar by the number of servings – don't forget that ingredients such as agave nectar and maple syrup are also sugars, and that chocolate contains about 30 per cent sugar. You could choose a smaller serving of a higher sugar recipe if you want to keep your sugar intake low.

Refined sugars are often produced with the aid of bone char, so are not vegan. You may wish to contact your supplier to find out if this is the case. Billington's unrefined sugars do not contain any animal products and are therefore suitable for vegans.

Glycemic Index (GI)

The GI value refers to the glycemic index of a sweetener, how quickly it releases its glucose. A lower value means a slower, steadier release, less likely to result in large blood sugar fluctuations.

Low GI 55 or less

Medium GI 56–69

High GI 70 or more

These categories depend on you and your sensitivity, for example if you are diabetic or insulin resistant you would need a lower GI than others. Your best indicator is how you feel after consuming different sweeteners.

types of sugar and sweetener

When a recipe states *sugar* your alternatives are:

- light raw cane sugar – includes some nutrients, GI 65
- white sugar – highly refined, no nutrients, GI 80
- maple sugar – what is left after making maple syrup, twice as sweet as sugar, GI 54
- date sugar – dehydrated ground dates, whole food so valuable source of nutrients, about 30% sweeter than sugar, won't melt, GI 30–60
- fructose/fruit sugar – refined fruit sugar, no nutrients, G1 17–25
- any of the brown sugars below.

When a recipe states *brown sugar* your alternatives are:

- evaporated cane juice/rapadura sugar/sucanat – dehydrated sugar cane juice, minimally processed, good flavour, contains many nutrients, GI 55
- unrefined coconut palm sugar – dehydrated palm flower sap, described by the World Health Organisation as 'the most sustainable sweetener in the world' as it is collected from a natural forest environment, without damage to the ecosystem, high in vitamins B and C, zinc, magnesium, potassium and iron, GI 35

- jaggery – unrefined sugar which can be made from palm sap or sugar cane juice, similar to both palm sugar and evaporated cane juice but has a unique and delicious flavour, considered to be of great medicinal benefit in Ayurvedic medicine, GI 35–55, depending on source
- muscovado/turbinado/dark raw cane sugar – similar types of sugar made from partially refined sugar cane, good flavour, moist, retain some nutrients, GI 65
- brown sugar – white sugar with molasses added to give colour and flavour, GI 80.

When a recipe states *icing sugar* your alternatives are:

(icing sugar is also known as confectioners' sugar or powdered sugar)

- unrefined icing sugar – raw sugar ground more finely, will add a light brown colour and slight molasses flavour, if you can't get this, you can grind your own raw sugar or evaporated cane juice in a coffee grinder, GI 65
- white refined icing sugar – smooth and white, good for icing but no nutrients, GI 80.

When a recipe states *maple syrup* or *agave nectar* your alternatives are:

- agave nectar – produced from the agave plant, 25-30% sweeter than sugar, retains some nutrients, good vegan alternative to honey, low GI 10-30
- maple syrup – made from the sap of maple trees, about 60% as sweet as sugar, delicious but distinctive flavour, GI 54
- concentrated fruit juice – typically apple or grape, made by boiling fruit juice until reduced to a syrup, GI n/a (but closer to refined sugars than fruit purees)
- brown rice syrup – made from cultured brown rice, about 50% as sweet as sugar, GI 25
- barley malt syrup – produced from sprouted barley, many nutrients, strong malty taste, about 50% as sweet as sugar, best combined with other sweeteners, GI 42
- fruit purees – whole foods, many nutrients, low GI (apple 40, prune 30, date 30–60)
- honey (see below) – can be 25-50% sweeter than sugar, GI 30 (raw), 75 (refined)
- golden syrup or corn syrup – highly refined sweeteners, good viscosity and flavour, GI 63 (golden syrup), 75 (corn syrup).

Honey

Honey is produced by bees, and is therefore something that vegans do not usually eat. However, I believe that when choosing what to eat you need to follow your heart, and my heart tells me that sharing raw, unprocessed honey with bees kept by small-scale, local beekeepers who tend their bees lovingly and with respect is not a bad thing.

Raw, local honey is rich in nutrients, has many medicinal qualities and racks up few food miles. I find it difficult to choose agave nectar or maple syrup – which has often been heated and refined, bottled thousands of miles away and transported by plane and truck – over raw, local honey.

But, as this is a vegan book, I have assumed that people would generally not choose honey, and I have usually suggested agave nectar or maple syrup instead. One exception is panforte (p. 180). Honey is a traditional ingredient in this recipe, and I have offered it as an option. If you are convinced by my argument, and have access to a local source of good, raw honey, feel free to substitute it for any of the wet sweeteners in this book, remembering that it can be a lot sweeter than sugar so you may need to use less than other syrups and nectars.

Other sweeteners

- stevia – not an artificial sweetener, but an extract from a herb which is 200–300 times sweeter than sugar, considered to be the only safe and natural sweetener on the market, slight aftertaste, GI 1
- artificial sweeteners (aspartame, sucralose, saccharin) – highly refined, no nutritional value, studies suggest health risks associated with these chemicals (such as an increased risk of stomach cancer), these sweeteners do not affect blood sugar so do not have a GI value
- sugar alcohols (xylitol, maltitol, sorbitol, isomalt, etc.) – highly refined sweeteners made from plant fibres, low in kilojoules compared to sugar, very low glycemic index so often marketed to diabetics, excessive consumption can cause bloating, flatulence and diarrhoea, GI 1–7.

grains

Without a doubt, whole grains are best. They contain fibre, antioxidants, iron, magnesium, vitamin E and the B group vitamins. Eating whole grains can reduce your risk of stroke, type 2 diabetes, heart disease, asthma, bowel cancer and high blood pressure. And they taste great! Cakes, biscuits and pastries made with wholemeal flour have a nutty flavour and a rich texture. They fill you up more, so you don't need to eat as much.

Sometimes a recipe calls for a lighter texture and, in this case, I use unbleached, organic flour. I never bother buying self-raising flour as you can always make it by adding baking powder to plain flour. Just add two teaspoons to each cup of flour (140 g wholemeal or 160 g white flour) and sift well.

Flours that are gluten free include buckwheat, amaranth, millet, quinoa, sorghum, rice, tapioca, maize meal, cornflour, potato starch and chickpea (besan) flour. If you want to use gluten-free flour, why not make up your own mixes rather than relying on the highly refined, very 'white' gluten-free flours you can buy commercially? Do read up on their properties, however, as each flour is different. Remember to balance the starchy, binding flours (cornflour, tapioca and potato starch) with the ones with a bit more flavour or nutritional value (buckwheat, millet, amaranth, quinoa, maize meal, sorghum, chickpea and rice flour). Try the mixes I have suggested on p. 45 and p. 85, but feel free to experiment with your own.

fats and oils

In my recipes, I have not been too specific about what kind of fat or oil to use. I tend to list either 'light oil' or 'dairy-free spread'. But which oil or dairy-free spread should you choose? If you want to make the healthiest choice it helps to understand a bit about different types of fat.

Depending on their molecular structure, fats and oils are grouped into three categories: saturated, monounsaturated and polyunsaturated. Fat molecules are made up of carbon, hydrogen and oxygen atoms, joined together by bonds. The saturated fats have all their bonds used up, they are full – 'saturated'. The unsaturated fats have spaces where extra atoms could go, they are not full – 'unsaturated'.

Saturated fats include animal fats and vegetable fats that are solid at room temperature, like coconut oil and palm oil. It used to be thought that all saturated fats raised 'bad' cholesterol (LDL) and lowered 'good' cholesterol (HDL), which could lead to heart disease. New research suggests that only animal fats do this and that the vegetable saturated fats, like coconut oil, may, in fact, confer a range of health benefits.

Monounsaturated and **polyunsaturated** fats are found in plant foods like olive, sunflower, safflower and soybean oils, avocadoes, nuts and seeds. They have slightly different molecular structures but it is thought that they both help increase HDL cholesterol and lower LDL cholesterol and therefore help prevent heart disease.

Choosing fats and oils

- Animal fats are saturated and can lead to heart disease.
- Most vegetable fats are unsaturated and help to maintain a healthy heart.
- Even the vegetable fats that are saturated (coconut and palm) offer health benefits.
- Hydrogenated fats contain trans fats which pose a health risk.
- When using oil, choose a good quality, light-flavoured oil such as rice bran, sunflower or canola. Try to find a brand that is GM free.
- When using dairy-free spread, look for a brand that is not hydrogenated and contains no trans fats.

Hydrogenation is a chemical process where extra hydrogen atoms are attached onto the molecules in unsaturated vegetable oils. They become 'saturated' with hydrogen. This has the effect of making the oils solid at room temperature, which is useful for manufacturers who want to make 'short' pastries, solid spreads or creamy icings more cheaply than if they used animal fats or good quality vegetable oils. Hydrogenation also increases the shelf life of products, which is great for manufacturers, but not for our health.

A result of hydrogenation is the formation of trans fat, which greatly increases the risk of heart disease. Indeed, trans fats are considered so damaging to health that some countries and regions have banned their use.

If you want to avoid hydrogenated fat, stay away from anything that mentions 'hydrogenated', 'partially hydrogenated', 'vegetable shortening' or 'trans fats', on the label. Better still, do your own baking, using a good quality vegetable oil or non-hydrogenated dairy-free spread.

thickeners

Arrowroot, cornflour, agar, kuzu, psyllium and lecithin are all products which can be used as a substitute for eggs and gelatine to thicken or gel a vegan dessert.

Arrowroot (tapioca flour) is a gluten-free flour which dissolves easily and thickens without becoming cloudy. For this reason it is really good for thickening fruit purees as it will not alter the colour of the fruit.

Cornflour (cornstarch) can be gluten free but some varieties have wheat added so check the label.

Both cornflour and arrowroot need to be dissolved in a little liquid first and mixed to a paste before adding to a hot liquid, then simmered for a few minutes to thicken and cook the flour. Both flours thicken easily without clumping.

Kuzu (kudzu) is made from the root of a Japanese plant similar to arrowroot. Kuzu thickens without flavour and gives a glossy, clear texture, and is said to have health benefits such as reducing blood pressure and helping with poor digestion. Use kuzu in a ratio of one part powder to five parts liquid. Mix to a paste with water, add to liquid and simmer until thick, whisking all the time.

Agar is a Japanese product made from seaweed used as a gelling agent. Very little is needed to produce a clear, good textured jelly but it is important to get the proportions of agar and liquid correct or the result could be a brick-like texture! I have experimented with agar flakes, sticks and powder and I find the powder easiest to control. The best ratio is one to two teaspoons of agar powder to one litre liquid. Sprinkle the agar on cold liquid and leave to soak for 15 minutes. Then heat the liquid and bring to the boil. Simmer for 15 minutes – the mixture may not visibly thicken, but do not worry, it will do so on cooling. Remove from the heat and allow to cool.

Psyllium comes from the seeds of the plantago plant. Psyllium husks are often used to add fibre to a diet and can also help to lower LDL ('bad') cholesterol. If you grind psyllium husks to a powder in a coffee grinder they can be added raw to a liquid to help thicken it. This makes them especially useful in raw food preparation.

Lecithin is found naturally in soybeans, vegetable oils, nuts, seeds and eggs. It contains phosphatidyl choline, inositol and Omega 3 essential fatty acids. Lecithin can lower cholesterol, disperse long-term fat stores in the body and improve memory and brain function. You can buy lecithin in granule form, derived from soybeans. If you grind the granules in a coffee grinder the powder can be added to creams and ice creams to give a thicker texture and a creamy mouthfeel.

nuts

Nuts are best consumed raw, as cooking can destroy nutrients. Nuts are seeds so have the potential to grow into a new plant. However, they contain enzyme inhibitors which prevent the nut sprouting until conditions are right. When it rains and the nut becomes saturated with water the enzyme inhibitors are destroyed and the nut can germinate. Mimicking this natural process, by soaking nuts for a few hours or overnight before using them, softens the nut and neutralises the enzyme inhibitors which can make the nuts easier to digest.

Roasting nuts

Although it is preferable to eat nuts raw, the flavour of roasted nuts is very special, and if they are going to be used in a cooked dessert anyway, you may as well do it.

To roast pecans, cashews or macadamias: place in a single layer on a baking tray in an oven set at about 170°C/325°F/ Gas 3 for 7–10 minutes until they look slightly browned and smell delicious.

To roast almonds: soak raw almonds in a bowl of boiling water for 5–10 minutes. Strain the almonds, then squeeze each one to pop the almond out of its skin. If it doesn't come out easily, soak in boiling water for a little longer. Leave the nuts to dry, then brown the almonds in the oven, as above.

To roast hazelnuts: place in a single layer on a baking tray in an oven set at about 170°C/325°F/Gas 3 for 7–10 minutes, then remove and pour onto a clean tea towel. Gather up the edges of the tea towel and rub the nuts briskly through the towel, until the skins rub off. Remove the nuts and empty the skins by shaking the tea towel outside.

chocolate, cacao and carob

Yes, vegans *can* eat chocolate! Good quality dark chocolate does not usually contain dairy products, but you do need to check the label. I have to confess to being a chocoholic. I love the stuff and, if possible, like to have some every day. But I am a discerning chocoholic. I only eat quality chocolate with 60–70% cocoa solids. And I don't gorge, I might have 20 or 30 g at a time. At these levels, I consider chocolate to be a health supplement.

Chocolate contains essential minerals like magnesium, potassium, copper and iron; phenylethylamine, the chemical produced when we are in love; anandamide, the bliss chemical; and bucketloads of antioxidants which mop up free radicals in our bodies and prevent disease.

Yes, it does also contain caffeine and its milder cousin, theobromine, chemicals which increase our focus and alertness but are often followed by a 'down' an hour or two later. However, the levels of caffeine in chocolate are much smaller than those in coffee and tea.

Cocoa powder is processed using heat and solvents which destroys many of the nutrients and antioxidants. Raw cacao, on the other hand, is cold pressed without solvents from the natural cocoa beans, then milled into powder. Raw cacao has all the same great nutrients as chocolate but loads more, as none have been destroyed during processing. It has approximately four times as many antioxidants as ordinary cocoa – scoring the highest level of all foods. This is why raw cacao has been hailed as a superfood.

Of course, raw cacao still contains theobromine and caffeine but some studies show the effects of these chemicals are less severe with raw cacao than chocolate.

Eating chocolate, raw cacao powder or whole cacao beans can certainly produce feelings of energy and wellbeing, and may also have long-term health benefits. However, as with all things, moderation is the key. Only you can judge the effects on your body of eating chocolate and cacao. If you feel jittery and can't sleep afterwards then maybe you should limit your intake or cut it out of your diet, perhaps replacing it with carob. But if you eat moderate amounts of chocolate, feel great, and don't suffer any ill effects, then I urge you to take your pleasure guiltlessly.

Please do think, however, about buying fairtrade chocolate and cocoa. Human rights abuses abound in the chocolate industry. We know that forced and abusive labour, including thousands of children, has been used in West African cocoa farms for years and yet companies are slow to act. Only chocolate and cocoa marked 'fairtrade' can guarantee that this does not occur. With fairtrade chocolate, forced and child labour are prohibited, farmers receive a price for their cocoa that meets their basic needs and environmentally sustainable production methods are encouraged.

Carob is often used as an alternative to chocolate. Carob has a pleasant, smoky flavour which is a little, but not much, like chocolate. It is sweeter than chocolate, contains no caffeine or theobromine and supplies a variety of vitamins and minerals, such as vitamins A, B, B2, B3 and D, calcium, phosphorus, potassium and magnesium, iron, manganese, barium, copper and nickel.

flavourings and colourings

I don't recommend artificial flavourings or colourings. In general I prefer to use natural foods to add flavour. But it is convenient to have a range of little bottles in your cupboard to enhance your baking. It is now possible to find natural and organic extracts such as vanilla, peppermint, orange, lemon and coffee flavourings, and natural food colourings.

Vanilla
The best flavour comes from fresh vanilla beans (see box below for how to use them), but they can be expensive so I tend to save them for dishes where the flavour really comes through, like vanilla ice cream and raw desserts. In some places it is possible to buy vanilla powder which is made from dehydrated, ground vanilla beans. When buying vanilla in a bottle, check the label and try to avoid brands that contain imitation vanilla, flavour, propylene glycol or preservative.

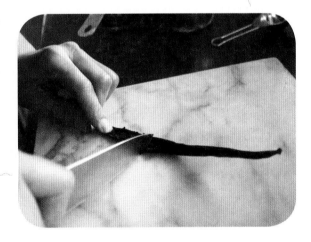

To scrape the seeds from a vanilla bean

1. Make a slit all the way down the bean with the tip of a sharp knife.
2. Open up the bean and lay it flat on a chopping board.
3. Using the flat blade of the knife, scrape from one end to the other, collecting all the sticky beans.
4. Add the beans to the liquid in your dish.
5. Use the empty pod to flavour icing sugar or agave nectar, just poke it in the jar, submerging the bean under the sugar or nectar.

Peppermint

The recipe for peppermint choc-chunk ice cream (p. 144) gives a method for shocking fresh peppermint to extract its flavour and colour. This method could be adapted to any recipe, by blending the shocked peppermint with whatever liquid you are using, and straining. This can be a bit time-consuming, but gives great results. As with vanilla, if buying essence, check the label for artificial additives.

Coffee

When a recipe suggests 'coffee essence', I prefer to brew some double-strength coffee, decaf coffee or coffee substitute, using a tablespoon of that instead of a teaspoon of essence. If this is likely to make the mixture too runny, reduce the other liquid in the recipe.

Orange, lemon, lime

When a recipe suggests citrus essence, I use the zest of the whole fruit plus the juice of half a fruit instead of a teaspoon of essence, reducing the other liquid in the recipe if necessary. As with vanilla, if buying essence, check the label for artificial additives.

Colours

For me the best colour in the world is rich chocolatey brown – and you don't need colouring for that, just the real, dark thing. But I know some of you out there like to spruce up your ice creams and frostings with a hint of colour. Maybe you can get hold of natural food colours where you live, but here are some ideas for doing it naturally.

- yellow/orange – a small pinch of turmeric
- red/pink – cherry, pomegranate or fresh beetroot juice
- blue/purple – blueberry juice
- green – a pinch of spirulina, or mint (see peppermint choc-chunk ice cream, p. 144).

salt

Last, but not least, the humble but essential salt. It is strange, but a little salt works wonders for a sweet dish. I usually include anything from a pinch to half a teaspoon in my recipes. I like to use Himalayan Pink Salt, a pure, hand-mined salt that contains over 80 natural minerals. Celtic sea salt is a good alternative.

the art of baking

Some cooking allows you to be spontaneous and inventive: soups, stews, sauces and curries, for example. You can sniff, taste, add a bit more of this or that, change the whole thing every time depending on your mood and what's in the fridge.

Baking is not like this. Believe me, I have munched my way through enough of my daughters' baking 'inventions' to know this. You can be creative in baking but you will probably have to test your attempts several times to get one that works. Many of the recipes in this book were born this way. I had a great idea, tried it, it was a disaster. I tweaked and changed things and had a couple more tries until finally it was just right. It takes dedication to make up dessert recipes from scratch.

So when you are making a dessert, at least for the first few times, you should probably stick to the recipe as it is written.

I don't want to inhibit your creativity, however, and once you know a few basic techniques you can experiment with variations. For example, once you know how to make ice cream, there are no end of flavour combinations you could come up with. The same goes for biscuits, cakes, crumbles, tarts and muffins. Stick to a basic recipe you know works and stamp your signature on it.

Tips for successful baking

- Read the recipe all the way through first.

- Preheat oven – check your oven temperature with a thermometer.

- Use recommended or similar size pan.

- Grease and line pans if recommended.

- Choose one set of measurements – cups or grams – and stick to it throughout the recipe. Teaspoon and tablespoon measurements can be used for both methods.

- Use accurate measuring equipment; measuring spoons rather than a normal teaspoon and well-calibrated measuring cups and jugs.

- If using scales, find some that measure down to 5 g. Digital scales are great, and can measure to 1 or 2 g, but they are expensive and use a lot of batteries. The old-fashioned sort your grandma used to have, with little weights, are excellent if you can get hold of some.

- When filling cups, level them with a flat knife, don't shake or bang the cup to settle the ingredients.

- When measuring liquids in a jug, read the measurement at eye level.

- Don't panic – if it all goes wrong you'll probably still be able to eat it, and you might have invented something amazing!

key

Everything in this book is free from animal ingredients: no eggs, no dairy, no gelatine or any other animal additives.

In addition, many of the recipes are suitable for people following gluten-free, wheat-free, raw, low sugar and nut-free diets. Each recipe is coded, and here is a full list.

GF   gluten free

WF   wheat free

R   raw

LS   low sugar

NF   nut free

Do be careful when using processed ingredients, for example, soy milk, baking powder, icing sugar, cornflour, etc. Many products contain added sugars and gluten-containing ingredients, and cannot guarantee they are nut free. Check the labelling carefully and, if you are in any doubt, contact the manufacturer for more information.

chapter one
cakes

'How can you make a cake without eggs and butter?'

I can't remember how many times I've been asked this question. The answer, of course, is 'Easy!' In fact, vegan cakes are much easier to make than their dairy and egg counterparts. There's no time-consuming creaming of butter that you forgot to take out of the fridge, or adding eggs little by little in case they curdle. In general a vegan cake is simply a matter of mixing all the wet and dry ingredients together separately, then combining the two and popping them in the oven.

In conventional recipes, butter adds flavour and moisture to a cake. Instead of butter, vegan cakes often use a clean-tasting oil, such as rice bran, sunflower or canola. Oil is easier to use, it mixes well with the other wet ingredients, like soy milk and vanilla. Dairy-free spread (preferably one without hydrogenated fat, colours or preservatives) can also be used, creamed as in a traditional cake recipe, and adds a little more flavour and moisture than oil. Lower fat cakes can be made with some or all of the oil replaced by nut butters or fruit purees.

Traditionally, eggs add moisture and act as a raising agent in cakes. Vegan cakes are kept moist by the oils, milks and fruits added to the recipe. Baking powder, bicarbonate of soda or a mixture of the two works well as a raising agent. If bicarbonate of soda is used, a little acid needs to be included, such as apple cider vinegar or citrus juice. This acid reacts with the alkaline soda and creates an instant 'whoosh'. For this reason, the wet ingredients (including the acid) should be mixed with the dry ingredients (including the soda) at the last minute and put in the oven immediately, so that all the little air bubbles created by the 'whoosh' can be captured and baked.

Tips for a successful cake

- Choose the right pan for the job and grease and/or line it according to instructions.

- Preheat the oven and assemble all your ingredients before mixing.

- Combine the wet and dry ingredients separately, then mix the two together at the last minute before putting them in the oven.

- Pour batter into prepared pans and level by tilting from side to side if the batter is runny, or gently smoothing with a palette knife or the back of a spoon if the batter is thicker. Put in the oven immediately.

- Set the timer for the minimum time specified. Don't open the door before this time is up as the air bubbles won't be set and the cake will collapse.

- After the minimum time has elapsed, check your cake. Have ready a wooden or metal skewer or toothpick, open the oven door and pull out the oven tray. If the cake has shrunk slightly away from the sides of the tin and bounces back when you press gently on top, it's ready. If you're not sure, poke the skewer right into the centre of the cake. If it comes out with bits of wet cake mix stuck to it, give it another five minutes and try again. When the cake is cooked the skewer will come out clean or slightly oily.

- If the skewer is coming out sticky but the surface of the cake looks too brown or the sides are shrinking too far from the sides of the pan, the oven is probably set too high. Cover the cake with foil and cook it for a few more minutes. Remember next time you make this cake to reduce the temperature by ten degrees.

- When you remove the cake from the oven, stand the tin on a wire cooling rack for between five and twenty minutes, then slide a palette knife around the edges of the cake and turn out on to the rack to finish cooling. Some cakes are cooled in the pan.

- Keep the cake in an airtight box and, if iced, in the refrigerator. Most cakes keep for two to three days. Fruit cake and chocolate torte keep longer.

Real Food Daily

I used to live in rural Lancashire in the northwest of England where, if you went to a restaurant asking for a vegan meal, they asked, 'What's a vegan?', looked at you as if you were barking mad when you told them and, if you were lucky, offered you a salad.

When I first visited Los Angeles in 2004 and discovered Real Food Daily, I thought I'd died and gone to heaven. A menu, pages long, filled with amazing, tasty vegan dishes and, an added bonus, all organic. When I returned in 2009 they had extended their restaurant and added a bakery. Heaven just got better. Rows and rows of delectable pastries, cookies and cakes of the sort a vegan believes they are never going to have the opportunity to eat. My two daughters and I shared five desserts – for breakfast! But we didn't need to feel guilty for, as well as being organic, the dishes contained healthy ingredients such as barley flour and natural sweeteners like maple syrup, agave nectar and fruit juices.

Ann Gentry, the creator of Real Food Daily, is a passionate food educator who has been working to raise the profile of vegan cooking in the USA for 25 years. As well as running Real Food Daily at two locations and constantly developing new recipes for the restaurant, Ann has written *The Real Food Daily Cookbook* and *Vegan Family Meals*. She frequently appears on television as an expert on vegan and organic cuisine.

The food at Real Food Daily is prepared using high quality organic produce and ingredients, and nearly everything is made from scratch. They use no meat, fish, fowl, dairy, eggs, butter, cholesterol, saturated fats from animals or animal by-products. Dishes are cooked with fresh herbs, spices, and sea salt, and condiments prepared in-house add a variety of gourmet flavours. Real Food Daily draws on Eastern health philosophies and Western nutritional recommendations, giving optimal nutrition and energy as well as a delicious taste experience.

Real Food Daily
514 Santa Monica Boulevard
Santa Monica
USA
Tel: 310 451 7544

Real Food Daily
414 N. La Cienega Boulevard
Los Angeles
USA
Tel: 310 289 9910

www.realfooddaily.com

Real Food Daily double chocolate layer cake with raspberry puree

This cake is moist and delicious – not too sweet, but rich and chocolatey. The raspberry flavour complements the chocolate beautifully. If you haven't got time to make the puree, just serve with fresh raspberries. You can use this sponge recipe as the basis for any chocolate cake or cupcake.

Grease and line the base of two 23 cm (9") pans with 4 cm (1½") high sides.

For the cake, sift the flour, cocoa powder, coffee powder, baking powder, bicarbonate of soda, and salt into a large bowl. Whisk the soy milk, maple syrup, oil, vanilla and vinegar in another bowl. Mix the wet and dry ingredients until just blended. Pour the batter into the prepared pans, dividing equally. Bake for 30-40 minutes, or until a skewer inserted into the centre of each cake comes out clean and the cakes begin to pull away from the sides of the pans. Cool in the pans on a metal cooling rack for 20 minutes. Turn out the cakes onto the rack and cool completely.

For the frosting, melt the chocolate chips in a bain-marie (see box below). Blend the tofu, cocoa, agave nectar and vanilla in a food processor until smooth and creamy. Add the melted chocolate to the tofu mixture and blend well, scraping down the sides of the bowl with a spatula if needed. Transfer the frosting to a bowl. Cover and refrigerate for about an hour, or until just firm enough to spread.

For the raspberry puree, combine the water and agar powder in a heavy saucepan and soak for 15 minutes. Bring to a simmer over high heat and then decrease the heat to medium-low and simmer for 15 minutes, stirring frequently. Transfer the mixture to a blender. Add the thawed raspberries and agave nectar and puree until smooth. Pour the puree into a bowl and stir in the fresh raspberries. Cover and refrigerate until the puree is cold. Stir before serving.

To assemble: place 1 cake layer on a platter, spread with 1½ cups of frosting. Top with the second cake layer. Spread the remaining frosting over the sides and top of the cake using a spatula. Serve the cake with raspberry puree.

Reprinted with permission from Ann Gentry, *The Real Food Daily Cookbook: Really Fresh, Really Good, Really Vegetarian*, Ten Speed Press, 2005.

Melting chocolate

It's important to melt chocolate gently, ideally in a bain-marie – a glass or ceramic bowl balanced over a small pan of gently simmering water. The bottom of the bowl should sit above the level of the simmering water, so that the heat from the steam melts the chocolate. Be careful not to drop any water into the chocolate as it is melting, otherwise it could 'seize', becoming stiff and granular.

Serves 12

CAKE

3 cups (450 g) barley flour

¾ cup (90 g) cocoa

¼ cup (30 g) instant decaffeinated coffee (or coffee substitute powder)

1½ teaspoons baking powder

1½ teaspoons bicarbonate of soda

1 teaspoon sea salt

2 cups (500 ml) soy milk

1½ cups (375 ml) maple syrup

¾ cup (180 ml) light oil, e.g. sunflower

1½ teaspoons vanilla extract

1 tablespoon cider vinegar

FROSTING

2 cups (400 g) chocolate chips

3 cups (720 g) firm silken tofu

1 cup (120 g) cocoa

⅓ cup (80 ml) agave nectar

2 teaspoons vanilla extract

RASPBERRY PUREE

¾ cup (180 ml) water

¼ teaspoon agar powder

2 cups (200 g) frozen raspberries, thawed

⅓ cup (80 ml) agave nectar

1 cup (100 g) fresh raspberries

Oven 170°C/325°F/Gas 3

coffee and walnut cake

This really is my favourite layer cake. Not as sweet as chocolate cake and with the lovely crunch of walnuts. I urge you to go the extra mile for fairtrade organic coffee if you can. It makes a big difference to the coffee farmers and their families. It works just as well with decaffeinated coffee or a coffee substitute. Just make sure you double the amount of coffee you would normally use to get the strength of flavour you need for the cake.

Grease and line the base of two 20 cm (8") round cake tins.

First, brew a cup of double-strength coffee or coffee substitute and leave to cool. In a small bowl or jug, whisk together the soy or rice milk and cider vinegar and leave for a few minutes before whisking in the oil, vanilla extract and coffee. Sift the flour, bicarbonate of soda, baking powder and salt into a large bowl. Add the sugar to the flour mixture. Mix the wet and dry ingredients together and beat until smooth. If the mixture is too dry, add a little more soy milk until the mixture drops easily off a spoon. Stir in the chopped walnuts. Fill the two sandwich tins evenly. Bake for 25-30 minutes until the sponge comes away slightly from the side of the tin. Leave the cakes in the tins for five minutes, then turn out onto a cooling rack. When cool, frost with coffee icing.

For the icing, beat the spread, salt and half a cup of icing sugar in a mixer until light and fluffy. (If you don't have a mixer, a food processor will do the job, but the result will not be as fluffy.) Add the remaining icing sugar, half a cup at a time, blending well after each addition. When all the sugar is incorporated, add the vanilla and coffee and blend well. The icing should be light, creamy and fluffy. If it is too firm, add more coffee or a little soy milk. If it becomes too runny, sift in a little more icing sugar.

Spread half the icing between the cooled cake layers and cover the top of the cake with the remainder. Decorate with walnut halves.

Serves 8-10

CAKE

3 tablespoons double-strength brewed coffee, or coffee substitute, cooled

1 cup (250 ml) soy or rice milk

1 tablespoon cider vinegar

⅓ cup (80 ml) light oil, e.g. sunflower

1 teaspoon vanilla extract

2 cups (280 g) wholemeal flour

1 teaspoon bicarbonate of soda

1 teaspoon baking powder

½ teaspoon salt

¾ cup (150 g) sugar

½ cup (50 g) walnuts, chopped, plus 8 walnut halves to decorate

COFFEE ICING

½ cup (100 g) dairy-free spread

pinch of salt

2 cups (320 g) icing sugar, sifted

1 teaspoon vanilla extract

3 tablespoons double-strength coffee, cooled

Oven 170°C/325°F/Gas 3

spiced carrot cake

Over the years this carrot cake has developed into the fine thing it is today. Moist, with just the right amount of spice. Wholesome, with just the right amount of creamy sweet icing. I flavour mine with wattle seed, an Australian native spice with a rich nutty, coffee-ish flavour. If you don't have it, don't stress. Why not try adding a spice from your neighbourhood, maybe five-spice, coriander or even a tiny pinch of cayenne?

Grease and line the base of a 23 cm (9") loaf tin.

For the cake, grate the carrots and soak the wattle seeds (if using). Soften the grated carrots in a large pan over a low heat for a few minutes, stirring every now and again. Allow to cool. In a small bowl or jug, whisk together the soy or rice milk and cider vinegar and leave for a few minutes, then add the oil and vanilla extract and whisk. Sift the flour, bicarbonate of soda, baking powder, spices and salt into a large bowl. Add the sugar to the flour mixture. Stir in the carrots, chopped walnuts and sultanas. Add the soaked wattle seeds to the soy milk mixture, then mix into the flour and beat until smooth. If the mixture is too dry, add a little more soy milk until the mixture just drops off a spoon. Fill the loaf tin and bake for 45-50 minutes until a skewer comes out clean. Leave the cake in the tin for 10-20 minutes, then turn out onto a cooling rack.

For the icing, beat the spread, vanilla extract, salt and a quarter cup (35g) of icing sugar in a mixer until light and fluffy. (If you don't have a mixer, a food processor will do the job, but the result will not be as fluffy.) Add three more quarter cups of the icing sugar, a quarter cup at a time, blending well after each addition. Add the cream cheese and lemon zest and mix. Depending on how runny your cream cheese is, add a further ¼ cup icing sugar and beat well. The icing should be light, creamy and fluffy. If it is too firm, add more soy milk. If it is too runny, add a little more icing sugar. When you are happy with the texture, taste the icing to see if you need to add a little more lemon zest or salt. Spread the icing on top of the cooled cake.

Serves 10-12

CAKE

2-3 medium (350 g) carrots, grated
½ teaspoon wattle seed, soaked in
   1 tablespoon hot water (optional)
1 cup (250 ml) soy or rice milk
1 tablespoon cider vinegar
⅓ cup (80 ml) light oil,
   e.g. sunflower
½ teaspoon vanilla extract
1 cup (140 g) wholemeal flour
1 cup (120 g) unbleached
   white flour
1 teaspoon bicarbonate of soda
1 teaspoon baking powder
1½ teaspoons cinnamon
½ teaspoon nutmeg
¼ teaspoon ground cardamom
¼ teaspoon ground ginger
½ teaspoon salt
⅔ cup (130 g) brown sugar
⅔ cup (70 g) walnuts, chopped
   coarsely
⅓ cup (55 g) sultanas or raisins

VANILLA CREAM-CHEESE ICING

¼ cup (50 g) dairy-free spread
½ teaspoon vanilla extract
¼ teaspoon salt
1-1¼ cups (140-175 g) icing sugar,
   sifted
¼ cup (50 g) vegan cream cheese
1 teaspoon lemon zest

Oven 170°C/325°F/Gas 3

squidgy fruit cake

'Squidgy' because the marzipan and fruits keep this cake sticky and moist all the way through. Be careful not to overcook this cake or you'll end up with 'Dry fruit cake' which isn't nearly as nice. It gets better the longer it is kept so – if you can – wait a few days before eating.

Line the base and sides of a 20 cm (8") deep, loose-based cake tin with a double layer of baking parchment, extending it about 5 cm (2") above the level of the pan.

The night before you make the cake, chop the marzipan into 1 cm (½") cubes and lay on a baking tray or freezer box in a single layer. Freeze overnight. Place the chopped apricots and pears in a large bowl with the sultanas and juice. Cover and leave to soak overnight.

In a small bowl or jug, gradually add the water to the flaxseeds or egg replacer and whisk until fluffy. Leave for 5 to 10 minutes to thicken.

Sift the flour, baking powder and salt into a large bowl. Add the ground almonds, lemon zest and sugar to the flour. Add the flaxseed mixture, oil and frozen marzipan to the soaked fruit and mix well. Then add the flour and mix thoroughly. It should be a heavy mixture, hard to stir. You'll know it's right if, when you hold up a spoonful of mixture, it slowly drops off the spoon. If it seems too dry, add a little more orange juice to loosen it a bit. Spoon into the baking tin and flatten down.

Bake for around 2 hours until cooked but not too dry. To test if the cake is ready, insert a skewer into the centre – if it comes out clean, it's cooked. If the cake starts to get too brown before it is cooked, cover with foil. When it's done, remove from oven and stand the tin on a wire cooling rack to cool. When cool, remove the cake from the tin and wrap in parchment and foil to keep it moist.

Serves 10-12

1 pack (250 g) marzipan
1 cup (150 g) dried pears, chopped
1 cup (150 g) dried apricots, chopped
1 cup (150 g) sultanas
½ cup (125 ml) orange juice
2 tablespoons ground flaxseeds (or if you don't have them, 3 teaspoons egg replacer)
½ cup (125 ml) water
1½ cups (200 g) wholemeal or spelt flour
1 teaspoon baking powder
½ teaspoon salt
⅓ cup (45 g) ground almonds
1 teaspoon lemon zest
½ cup (100 g) firm-packed brown sugar
½ cup (125 ml) light oil, e.g. sunflower
1-2 tablespoons orange juice

Oven 140°C/275°F/Gas 1

hazelnut cupcakes with mocha mousse filling

If you don't already have a copy of Vegan Cupcakes Take Over the World *by Isa Chandra Moskowitz and Terry Hope Romero, shame on you. As they have defined the vegan cupcake, there is simply no point in me trying to compete. So I asked Isa and Terry if I could reproduce one of my favourites from their book. They gladly agreed to share. This recipe should convince you to go immediately and buy a copy of their book.*

Line a muffin tin with 12 paper liners.

For the cupcakes, grind the hazelnuts finely in a food processor or coffee grinder. Sift the ground hazelnuts, flour, baking powder, bicarbonate of soda, cinnamon, nutmeg and salt into a large bowl. In a small bowl whisk together the rice milk and ground flaxseeds. Add the oil, maple syrup, brown sugar and extracts to the milk mixture and beat well. Add the wet ingredients to the dry, mixing until smooth. Pour into cupcake liners, filling them two-thirds full. Bake 22-24 minutes until a skewer inserted into the centre comes out clean. Cool completely on a wire rack before filling.

For the mocha mousse filling, chop the chocolate and melt it in a bain-marie (see p. 27). Dissolve the coffee or substitute in a small amount of boiling water. In a food processor, blend all the ingredients, except the chocolate, until very smooth. Then, add the melted chocolate to the mixture and continue to blend, scraping down the sides of the bowl with a spatula now and again. Transfer the mousse to a bowl and refrigerate for about an hour to firm up.

TO DECORATE THE CAKES

Prepare the chocolate ganache (p. 169) and chop the hazelnuts coarsely. Fit a piping bag with a wide nozzle and fill it with the mocha mousse filling.

Use a finger to poke deep holes in the top of each cupcake. Fill each hole with as much mousse as you can. Remove any excess from the top of the cake.

Spread the ganache over the top of the cupcake and sprinkle with chopped hazelnuts. Chill in the fridge to set the ganache.

Reprinted with permission from Isa Chandra Moskowitz and Terry Hope Romero, *Vegan Cupcakes Take Over the World*, Marlowe & Company, 2006.

Makes 12

CUPCAKES

⅓ cup (45 g) hazelnuts

1 cup plus 2 tablespoons (135 g)
    unbleached white flour

1 teaspoon baking powder

¼ teaspoon bicarbonate of soda

½ teaspoon ground cinnamon

¼ teaspoon ground nutmeg

½ teaspoon salt

⅔ cup (160 ml) rice milk or nut milk

1 tablespoon ground flaxseeds

⅓ cup (80 ml) light oil, e.g. sunflower

¼ cup (60 ml) maple syrup

½ cup (100 g) brown sugar

1 teaspoon vanilla extract

MOCHA MOUSSE FILLING

1½ bars (150 g) chocolate

⅔ cup (160 g) silken tofu

2 tablespoons soy milk

1-2 tablespoons agave nectar or
    maple syrup, to taste

2 teaspoons instant coffee, or coffee
    substitute

2 teaspoons hazelnut liqueur
    (optional)

1 teaspoon vanilla extract

TO FINISH

½ batch chocolate ganache (p. 169)

½ cup (70 g) toasted hazelnuts
    (see p. 15)

Oven 180°C/350°F/Gas 4

chocolate torte

This is divine – a gluten-free torte frosted with a creamy, chocolatey, not-too-sweet tofu frosting. Don't expect the torte to rise like a sponge, it's moist and dense and will stay flat, or even sink a little. This isn't a failure, just top with frosting, it will taste wonderful. The torte will keep well in the refrigerator for up to three days, if you can leave it that long.

Grease and line the base of a 23 cm (9") round cake tin.

To make the torte, sift the cocoa, flour, baking powder, bicarbonate of soda and salt into a bowl. Add the sugar. In a food processor or blender combine the tofu, maple syrup, oil, vanilla and cider vinegar and mix thoroughly until creamy. Add the coffee and blend again. Add this wet mixture to the bowl of sifted flour and whisk until smooth. Pour batter into tin and spread evenly. Bake for 20 minutes or until the cake comes a little away from the sides of the tin. Cool in tin. When cool, invert onto a plate and peel off the baking parchment.

For the frosting, melt the chocolate in a bain-marie (see p. 27). In a food processor, blend the rest of the ingredients until very smooth. When the chocolate has melted add it to the mixture and blend, scraping down the sides of the bowl with a spatula now and again. Transfer the mousse to a bowl and refrigerate for about an hour until it thickens. Then spread a thick layer on top of the torte.

Serves 6-8

TORTE

¼ cup (35 g) cocoa

1 cup (135 g) gluten-free flour mix 1 (p. 45) or other gluten-free flour

½ teaspoon baking powder

½ teaspoon bicarbonate of soda

¼ teaspoon salt

½ cup (100 g) sugar

½ cup (120 g) silken tofu

¼ cup (60 ml) maple syrup

¼ cup (60 ml) light oil, e.g. sunflower

1 teaspoon vanilla extract

1 teaspoon cider vinegar

2 tablespoons double-strength coffee, or coffee substitute

FROSTING

½ cup (120 g) silken tofu

2 tablespoons maple syrup

2 tablespoons soy or rice milk

1 teaspoon vanilla extract

1 bar (100 g) chocolate

Oven 180°C/350°F/Gas 4

vitality cake

GF LS

A version of this cake was introduced to me by a friend who called it 'menopause cake' as it contains so many beneficial nutrients for women at that stage of life. I chose 'vitality cake' to focus on the positive health benefits of the ingredients for women – and men – of all ages. This cake contains no added fat or sugars, only the healthy plant oils in nuts and seeds and natural fruit sugars. Because of this it won't keep as well as fruit cake, so best eaten within two to three days. Last time I made it I was in a hurry and discovered that it is very tasty eaten while still warm.

Grease and line the base of a 23 cm (9") round cake tin, or 23 cm x 30 cm (9" x 12") rectangular tin.

To make the date puree, put the dates in a saucepan with the water and simmer for ten minutes or until meltingly soft. Cool then puree in a blender or food processor.

Sift the flour, baking powder, cocoa or carob powder and spices. Add the fruit, seeds and nuts.

Mix in the date puree and the lemon and orange juice. If it still seems a bit too stiff and dry, add a little soy or rice milk. Spread in the prepared pan and bake for about 1-1¼ hours until firm on top and a skewer comes out clean. Remove from oven and stand the tin on a wire rack. Once cool remove the cake from the tin and wrap in parchment and foil to keep moist.

Serves 12-16

DATE PUREE

2 cups (250 g) stoned, chopped
   dates

1¼ cups (300 ml) water

CAKE

1¼ cups (185 g) whole-wheat flour
   or gluten-free flour mix 1 (p. 45)

1 teaspoon baking powder

1 tablespoon cocoa or
   carob powder

1 teaspoon cinnamon

1 teaspoon mixed spice

¼ teaspoon nutmeg

3½ cups (500 g) any dried fruit:
   sultanas, raisins, chopped
   apricots or prunes (if the fruit is
   hard, soak for a couple of hours
   in warm water)

½ cup (75 g) any seeds: sunflower,
   sesame, linseed, pumpkin

½ cup (80 g) ground almonds or
   other nuts

juice 1 orange and 1 lemon

Oven 140°C/275°F/Gas 1

black forest gateau

Okay, this is probably not what you are expecting from a black forest gateau. Gluten free. Low sugar. Raw. But if there's one dessert that's going to convince the wary that raw food can be decadent and delicious, this is it. Chocolate, cherries, cream, macadamia fudge crumble crust . . . who could argue with that? It does take a bit of time to put together, but – for a celebratory feast – is so worth it. There are lots of stages so read through the recipe carefully before you start, and remember to leave enough time for soaking and chilling.

A couple of hours before you're ready to start, soak the cashews for the cream and the hazelnuts for the filling. Then assemble all your ingredients in the order you'll need them. I recommend making the chocolate, cashew cream and chocolate sauce first, then the crumble crust and the hazelnut filling and finally assemble everything.

Mix up a batch of raw chocolate and spread it thinly on a tray lined with baking parchment. Put in the freezer to set. Make the cashew cream and the raw chocolate sauce and chill.

For the macadamia fudge crumble crust, put the macadamias, cacao powder, carob powder, vanilla seeds and salt in a food processor and blend to crumbs. Add the dates and agave nectar and process until the mixture starts to come together in a ball. Divide the mixture in two. Press half into the base of an 18 cm (7") loose-bottomed cake tin, with sides at least 10 cm (4") deep. Reserve the other half in the fridge.

For the chocolate-hazelnut mousse, first make the hazelnut milk. This isn't as hard as it sounds. Just blend the soaked hazelnuts with the water at high speed until the nuts are as fine as they will go. Then strain the mixture into a large jug or bowl through some muslin or cheesecloth if you have it, or a fine sieve. Squeeze to get as much milk out as you can, and discard the nut fibre. Put the cacao, carob, vanilla seeds, dates, maple syrup and salt in the blender, and add the hazelnut milk gradually as you blend. When the mixture is smooth and you have added all the milk, add the lecithin, coconut oil and psyllium powder with the blender still running. Pour the mousse into the cake tin. Chill until set.

Spread the halved, pitted cherries over the top of the mousse, then pour the cashew cream over the cherries. Break the remaining macadamia fudge crumble crust into small pieces with your fingers and sprinkle over the top of the cake. Drizzle the chocolate sauce over the crumble. Break the raw chocolate into chunks and poke in the cake. Decorate with the whole cherries. Set in the freezer for at least an hour or chill in the fridge overnight.

When you are ready to serve, carefully push the base of the cake tin up. Depending on the thickness of your mousse and cream, and how long you have left the gateau to chill, it may collapse a little as you remove the sleeve, but it won't matter, it will taste divine.

Serves 12

1 batch raw chocolate (p. 187)
1 batch cashew cream (p. 167)
½ batch raw chocolate sauce (p. 170)
1 cup (about 225 g) fresh black
  cherries, halved and pitted
6-8 whole cherries, for decoration

MACADAMIA FUDGE CRUMBLE CRUST

1½ cups (200 g) macadamias
¼ cup (30 g) cacao powder
2 tablespoons carob powder
seeds of 1 vanilla bean
pinch of salt
½ cup (100 g) medjool dates,
  chopped
1 tablespoon agave nectar

CHOCOLATE-HAZELNUT MOUSSE

1 cup (140 g) hazelnuts, soaked
1½ cups (375 ml) water
¼ cup (30 g) cacao powder
2 tablespoons carob powder
seeds of 1 vanilla bean
½ cup (100 g) medjool dates,
  chopped
2 tablespoons maple syrup
pinch of salt
1 tablespoon soy lecithin (see p. 14)
¼ cup (60 ml) coconut oil
1 teaspoon psyllium powder
  (see p. 14)

three kinds of vanilla cake
basic

This is a foundation sponge which can be used for all kinds of recipes: cupcakes, layer cakes, loaf cakes, trifles or tiramisu. This quantity will make 12 small cupcakes, one small (23 cm/9") loaf tin, (23 cm/9") round tin or (23 cm/9") square tin. Double the quantity if you want a two-layer sandwich cake.

Grease and line pan with baking parchment. If using a muffin tin, line with 12 paper liners.

Sift the flour, bicarbonate of soda, baking powder and salt into a large bowl. In a smaller bowl, or large jug, mix the milk and cider vinegar and leave for a few minutes to thicken slightly. Whisk in the oil, sugar and vanilla extract. Add the wet ingredients to the dry and stir gently with a spatula to incorporate all the flour into the mixture. Pour the batter into the tin and roll it gently to level the mixture.

Bake according to the times given below until the cake has risen, turned golden and doesn't wobble too much when you give it a little shake. Take the cake out of the oven and check if it is done by inserting a skewer into the centre of the cake – if it comes out with sticky stuff on it, cook a little longer. Try not to overbake or the sponge will be dry and the edges crispy! Cool in the tin for 5 to 10 minutes, then remove from tin and cool on a wire rack.

1½ cups (240 g) unbleached flour
½ teaspoon bicarbonate of soda
1 teaspoon baking powder
½ teaspoon salt
1 cup (250 ml) soy milk
1 tablespoon cider vinegar
⅓ cup (80 ml) light oil,
   e.g. sunflower
⅔ cup (130 g) sugar
1 teaspoon vanilla extract

Oven 170°C/325°F/Gas 3

BAKING TIMES
Cupcakes: 20-25 minutes.

23 cm (9") sandwich or square tin: 25-30 minutes.

23 cm (9") loaf tin: 35-40 minutes.

OPTIONS
Chocolate: substitute ⅓ cup of the flour with cocoa.

Lemon: add the zest of one lemon to batter, replace vanilla with 1 tablespoon lemon juice or ¼-½ teaspoon lemon extract.

Orange: add the zest of one orange to batter, replace vanilla with 1 tablespoon orange juice or ¼-½ teaspoon orange extract.

Almond: substitute ½ cup of the flour with ground almonds, add ¼-½ teaspoon almond extract.

wheat free

Here is a wheat-free (but not gluten-free) version of the basic vanilla sandwich. It is also soy free. This is a lighter, slightly drier, less sweet version of the basic vanilla sandwich recipe – good for trifles and tiramisu, or for cupcakes or layer cakes with lots of frosting. It has a more 'wholemeal' look and flavour, and is definitely more nutritious!

Grease and line tin with baking parchment. If using muffin tin, line with 12 paper liners.

Sift the barley flour, bicarbonate of soda, baking powder and salt into a large bowl. In a smaller bowl, or large jug, mix the cider vinegar and milk. Rice milk won't thicken like soy milk, so you can whisk in the oil, maple syrup, vanilla extract and sugar straightaway. Add the wet ingredients to the dry and stir gently with a spatula to incorporate all the flour into the mixture. Pour the batter into the tin and roll it gently to level the mixture.

Bake according to the times given on p. 43 until the cake has risen, turned golden and doesn't wobble too much when you give it a little shake. Take the cake out of the oven and check if it is done by inserting a skewer into the centre of the cake – if it comes out with sticky stuff on it, cook a little longer. But try not to overbake or the sponge will be dry and the edges crispy! Cool in tin for 5 minutes, then remove from tin and cool on a wire rack.

Baking times and options as basic cake.

2¼ cups (325 g) barley flour

½ teaspoon bicarbonate of soda

1 teaspoon baking powder

½ teaspoon salt

1 tablespoon cider vinegar

1 cup (250 ml) rice milk

¼ cup (60 ml) light oil,
     e.g. sunflower

¼ cup (60 ml) maple syrup

1 teaspoon vanilla extract

½ cup (100 g) sugar

Oven 170°C/325°F/Gas 3

Grease and line tin with baking parchment. If using muffin tin, line with 12 paper liners.

Sift the flour, bicarbonate of soda, baking powder and salt into a large bowl. In a smaller bowl, or large jug, mix the milk and cider vinegar and leave for a few minutes to thicken slightly. Then whisk in the oil, sugar, agave nectar and vanilla extract. Add the wet ingredients to the dry and stir gently with a spatula to incorporate all the flour into the mixture. Pour the batter into the tin and roll it gently to level the mixture.

Bake according to the times given on p. 43 until the cake has risen, turned golden and doesn't wobble too much when you give it a little shake. Take the cake out of the oven and check if it is done by inserting a skewer into the centre of the cake – if it comes out with sticky stuff on it, cook a little longer. But try not to overbake or the sponge will be dry and the edges crispy! Cool in tin for 5 minutes, then remove from tin and cool on a wire rack.

Baking times and options as basic cake.

2 cups (280 g) gluten-free flour mix 1 (see below) or other gluten-free flour
1 teaspoon bicarbonate of soda
1 teaspoon baking powder
½ teaspoon salt
1 cup (250 ml) soy milk
1 tablespoon cider vinegar
½ cup (125 ml) light oil, e.g. sunflower
½ cup (100 g) sugar
¼ cup (60 ml) agave nectar or maple syrup
1 teaspoon vanilla extract

Oven 170°C/325°F/Gas 3

Gluten-free flour mix 1 (great for cakes)

½ cup (65 g) cornflour

½ cup (60 g) tapioca flour

½ cup (90 g) potato starch

½ cup (60 g) rice flour

¼ cup (35 g) chickpea (besan) flour

¼ cup (40 g) white sorghum or buckwheat flour

Measure all the flours into a big bowl and mix well.

chapter two
teatime treats

I am fortunate indeed to have lived in two countries where it is considered appropriate, nay necessary, for the day to include a pause for a cup of tea and a taste of something sweet. I was born and brought up in England where, as everyone knows, 4 pm afternoon tea is a national institution, and the English teashop a cultural treasure. Now I live in Australia where there are not one but two daily opportunities for 'a little something'. It is not unusual for Australians to have a break for morning tea at around 10 am and another one for afternoon tea at around 4 pm or 5 pm. Gatherings of friends frequently come with the invitation, 'Bring a plate of morning/afternoon tea to share'.

My definition of a teatime treat is something not quite as big as a cake, nor as small as a sweet. It should be robust enough to be packed in a box and carried in a basket to a park or beach; small enough to hold easily in the hand; and plentiful enough to share with lots of friends.

I'd visited Melbourne twice before. People kept asking me, 'Have you been to Las Vegan Nirvana?' I couldn't believe that I hadn't explored such an intriguing sounding place, so on my third visit I was determined to do so. I arrived on a Friday evening after an eleven-hour train journey from Adelaide. I was starving, so, suitcase and all, I boarded a tram to Collingwood, one of Melbourne's trendy inner suburbs. Smith Street is home to an eclectic mix of cafes and shops focusing on books, music and fashion. Not quite as genteel as big sister Brunswick Street, and still a bit daggy in places, Smith Street has a more comfortable, friendly feel – like your favourite old cardi. Smith Street also seems to be fast becoming a vegan hub, with Las Vegan Nirvana, Trippy Taco (a vegan-friendly Mexican cafe) and Ethical Wares (selling beautiful, made-to-order vegan shoes).

I arrived at Las Vegan Nirvana, looking like I was planning on moving in, parked my suitcase and made myself comfortable in the cosy, colourful dining room. I took some time to peruse the menu full of wholesome and yummy vegan dishes – all made from scratch in their own kitchen and organic where possible. Many dishes were also gluten free. I eventually chose the Nirvana lentil burger, a tasty homemade pattie in a homemade bun with masses of salad. Just what I needed. But – and I always do this – I was then too full for dessert, which was really what I came for. I'd heard that muffins were a speciality at Las Vegan, so I took away two for breakfast the next day: a sour cherry and a chocolate. They were both gorgeous, but the cherry muffin was definitely the winner and I have procured the recipe for your delight.

Las Vegan Nirvana started in 1999 as a vegan bakery, but has been running as a cafe since 2005.

Las Vegan Nirvana
22 Smith Street
Melbourne
Australia
Tel: 03 9415 9001 or 0433 457 591

www.lasvegan.com.au

Las Vegan Nirvana

Las Vegan sour cherry muffins

These muffins are big and sticky and tasty, but surprisingly lower in fat and sugar than usual varieties. You will need a jar of pitted sour cherries, which usually come from Eastern Europe and can be found in continental delicatessens and some supermarkets.

Line a muffin tin with 12 paper liners.

Strain the cherries, reserving the juice for the muffin mix and the glaze.

For the muffins, in a food processor, coarsely grind the almonds. Sift the flour, bicarbonate of soda and cinnamon into a large mixing bowl. Add the sugar and almonds to the flour and mix well. Mix the cherry juice, apple juice, oil and vanilla in a small bowl. Add this mixture to the dry ingredients. Fold together carefully – do not overmix – and stir in the cherries. Add extra apple juice if needed; you are looking for a fairly loose but not too runny consistency.

Pour a generous amount of batter into each liner – I find it useful to use a ⅓ cup (5 tablespoons) measure for this, which seems to be about the right amount – and bake for 25-30 minutes until a skewer comes out clean. Do not over bake.

For the glaze, heat the cherry juice and sugar together in a small pan. Bring to the boil, then remove from the heat. Brush the muffins with the syrup immediately after baking, then cool on a wire rack.

Makes 12

MUFFINS
¼ cup (35 g) almonds
2½ cups (400 g) unbleached
    white flour
½ teaspoon bicarbonate of soda
½ teaspoon cinnamon
1¼ cups (125 g) sugar
½ cup (125 ml) cherry juice
1 cup (250 ml) apple juice
½ cup (125 ml) light oil,
    e.g. sunflower
½ teaspoon vanilla extract
1 cup (225 g) pitted sour cherries

GLAZE
¼ cup (60 ml) cherry juice
2 tablespoons (25 g) sugar

Oven 180°C/350°F/Gas 4

double fudge pecan brownies

This recipe comes from the very first vegan dessert book I owned, Simple Treats *by Ellen Abraham. The page in my book is now covered with chocolate smudges and little notes like 'great' and 'make double'. I've altered the recipe over the years, mainly to make it gluten free – and to double it! It is, without doubt, the best brownie recipe in the world. The secret is sweet potato – but don't tell anyone until after they have declared it delicious. I love these brownies warm with vanilla ice cream.*

Grease and line the base of a 20 cm x 30 cm (8" x 12") rectangular tin.

Prepare the sweet potato puree and leave to cool.

In a large bowl sift the flour, cocoa, baking powder and salt into a bowl and stir in the nuts, chocolate chips and sugar. In a smaller bowl or jug whisk together the oil, maple syrup, vanilla, soy milk and sweet potato puree. Add the wet ingredients to those in the large bowl and stir well. The batter should be moist enough to pour into the pan. If it is too stiff, stir in a little more soy milk.

Pour the batter into the tin. Bake for 30-35 minutes until just done. This is when you can gently push the top of the cake with your finger and it springs back, NOT when a skewer comes out clean. For this cake, you want the inside to remain slightly moist.

Cool in the tin. Cut into 12-15 pieces.

Adapted with permission from Ellen Abraham, *Simple Treats: a wheat-free, dairy-free guide to scrumptious baked goods*, Book Publishing Company, 2003

Makes 12-15

½ cup sweet potato puree (about 150 g sweet potato, peeled, boiled and mashed)

1½ cups (200 g) gluten-free flour mix 1 (p. 45), or other gluten-free flour

1 cup (120 g) cocoa

¾ teaspoon baking powder

½ teaspoon salt

½ cup (50 g) pecans, or walnuts (optional)

½ cup (100 g) chocolate chips, or chopped chocolate

1 cup (200 g) sugar

½ cup (125 ml) light oil, e.g. sunflower

½ cup (125 ml) maple syrup

2 teaspoons vanilla extract

¾ cup (180 ml) soy milk

Oven 170°C/325°F/Gas 3

steve's flapjacks

GF LS

Steve has been making these for years, without a recipe. They vary each time but are always full of spices and big chunks of fruit, nuts and seeds. Unlike many flapjack recipes, they are not at all greasy. Everybody loves them. I finally pinned him down to making a batch with me standing by measuring and weighing each ingredient.

Grease and line the base of a 20 cm (8") square tin.

Weigh out and chop all the ingredients before you start because once you have melted the fat and sweeteners you need to add everything quickly.

Put the dairy-free spread in a large, heavy-based pan and melt over a low heat. Add the sugar and allow it to dissolve. Then add the syrups. When the mixture is all runny, remove from heat and stir in all the other ingredients except the rolled oats.

Add most of the oats and stir well to combine. If there is still any liquid at the bottom, stir in some more oats. You want a moist but not too wet mixture. The exact quantity of oats you need depends on how much liquid they will absorb. Quick porridge oats are probably more porous than steel-cut oats, so you may not need as many.

Put the mixture into the prepared tin and press down well. Bake in the centre of the oven for about 20-25 minutes. They are done when the top looks and feels dry. The middle is supposed to stay a bit sticky and you don't want them to brown too much – better to undercook than burn these.

Remove from the oven and stand the tin on a wire cooling rack. After about 10 minutes, loosen from the edge of the tin and mark into 12 pieces. Cool in the tin. Flapjacks keep for a week or more in an airtight tin.

Makes 12

⅓ cup (65 g) dairy-free spread

⅓ cup (65 g) sugar

2 tablespoons agave nectar or maple syrup

1 tablespoon brown rice syrup or barley malt syrup

¾ cup (75 g) walnuts or brazil nuts or a mixture, chopped coarsely

¼ cup (35 g) each of pumpkin, sunflower and sesame seeds

½ cup (80 g) raisins or sultanas

¼ cup (35 g) each of dates and dried apricots, chopped coarsely

1 teaspoon cinnamon

½ teaspoon mixed spice

2-2½ cups (200-250 g) rolled oats

Oven 170°C/325°F/Gas 3

cinnamon apple raisin muffins

This recipe is gluten free and refined sugar free (with an optional sugary topping for you sweet tooths out there). It includes bags of wholesome ingredients and tastes divine just out of the oven with a hot cuppa.

Grease a 6 or 12-hole muffin tin, or use paper muffin liners.

Sift the flour, baking powder, bicarbonate of soda and spices. Stir in the ground nuts. Whisk the oil, maple syrup or agave nectar, vanilla and rice milk together and add to the dry ingredients. Stir lightly together, don't over mix. Stir in the apples and raisins. If the mixture seems too dry, add a couple more tablespoons of rice milk.

Fill each cup in the muffin tin about three-quarters full. If using, sprinkle with the cinnamon sugar topping.

Bake for 18-22 minutes until risen and firm on top. Cool for a few minutes in the tin, then run a palette knife around each muffin and lift out on to a cooling rack.

**Makes 6 enormous or
12 average-sized muffins**

1½ cups (200 g) gluten-free flour mix 1 (p. 45) or other gluten-free flour
1 teaspoon baking powder
½ teaspoon bicarbonate of soda
1½ teaspoons cinnamon
¼ teaspoon nutmeg
½ cup (70 g) almonds or hazelnuts, ground
¼ cup (60 ml) light oil, e.g. sunflower
¼ cup (60 ml) maple syrup or agave nectar
1 teaspoon vanilla extract
½ cup (125 ml) rice milk
⅓ cup (55 g) raisins
2 apples, peeled, cored and chopped

**CINNAMON SUGAR TOPPING
(OPTIONAL)**
Mix together:
2 tablespoons brown sugar
½ teaspoon cinnamon

Oven 180°C/350°F/Gas 4

anzac biscuits

These biscuits were invented during World War I by the wives, mothers and girlfriends of Australian soldiers who wanted to send nutritious food to their loved ones, containing ingredients that would survive the long journey by sea. They came up with rolled oats, sugar, flour, coconut, butter, golden syrup and bicarbonate of soda. Because of the war, eggs were not readily available, making this recipe easy to veganise. My recipe is slightly less sweet than the traditional recipe, as well as being lower in fat and wheat free. There's also an option of adding extra nutritional value with a few nuts or seeds, thus pleasing almost everyone.

Cover a large baking tray with baking parchment.

Mix the oats, coconut, flours and salt. Add nuts or seeds if using.

Melt the sugar, golden syrup and oil in a small pan. When it is melted boil the kettle and mix the bicarbonate of soda with two tablespoons of boiling water. Stir quickly and add to the pan. As it bubbles up, pour over the dry ingredients and mix together.

Drop teaspoon-size balls onto the baking tray and flatten down. Bake for 10-12 minutes until golden brown. Remove from oven and cool on the tray.

Makes 14-16

1 cup (100 g) rolled oats
½ cup (50 g) desiccated coconut
½ cup (70 g) brown rice flour
½ cup (60 g) tapioca flour
pinch of salt
handful chopped nuts or seeds
 (optional)
½ cup (100 g) sugar
2 tablespoons golden syrup
¼ cup (60 ml) light oil (coconut oil
 is nice if you have it)
1 teaspoon bicarbonate of soda
2 tablespoons boiling water

Oven 170°C/325°F/Gas 3

almond and lemon cantucci

When we were in Siena, Italy, we saw these delicious-looking biscuits everywhere, but as they weren't vegan we couldn't try them. I vowed to create a vegan version when we got home, and here they are. Some people call these biscotti. This simply means biscuits in Italian and derives from the Latin word meaning 'twice baked'. Cantucci is the more accurate term for these almond-flavoured slices from Tuscany, which are often served with, and dipped in, a glass of the local fortified wine, Vin Santo. Cantucci keep for several weeks in an airtight container, and make great Christmas presents.

Grease and line a large baking tray.

Cook the apple with a little water until it softens, then mash to a puree. (If you don't have time for this step, you can use bottled apple sauce.)

Sift the flours, baking powder and salt. Mix the oil, extracts and half a cup (125ml) of the apple puree in a jug or small bowl. Add the liquid, sugar, lemon zest and whole almonds to the flour and mix to a soft dough. If too dry, sprinkle tablespoons of water one at a time until the dough comes together. Divide into two and roll into log shapes, about 5 cm (2") across and 2 cm (1") high.

Place on the baking sheet. Bake for 25 minutes. Remove from oven and leave to cool for 5 minutes. Cut each log diagonally into slices about 2 cm (1") thick, using a sharp knife so you can cut easily through the whole almonds. Lay the slices on their sides and bake for 15 minutes, then turn the slices over and bake for a further 15 minutes until golden brown and quite firm. Cool on a wire rack.

Makes 20-24

1 large apple, peeled and chopped
1 cup (160 g) white flour
1 cup (140 g) wholemeal flour
2 teaspoons baking powder
¼ teaspoon salt
3 tablespoons light oil,
  e.g. sunflower
1 teaspoon vanilla extract
2-3 drops almond extract
¾ cup (150 g) sugar
1 teaspoon lemon zest
1 cup (140 g) almonds, raw,
  skins left on

Oven 170°C/325°F/Gas 3

devon scones with jam and cream

Why should vegans miss out on the quintessential English afternoon tea of a freshly brewed pot of tea with homemade scones, jam and cream? Secrets of a really puffy, light scone:

- *sift the baking powder and flour a few times, holding the sieve high to incorporate as much air as possible*
- *mix the liquid in gradually with a fork*
- *handle the dough as little as possible – I never use a rolling pin, I just pat the dough into shape with the flat of my hand*
- *cut rounds with a sharp cookie cutter, avoiding too many scraps as the ones you re-roll will not rise as well.*

Grease a baking tray.

Mix the soy milk and vinegar and allow to thicken for a few minutes. Sift the flour, baking powder, bicarbonate of soda and salt several times to aerate the flour and incorporate the raising agents. Mix in the sugar, then rub in the fat until the mixture looks like breadcrumbs.

Make a well in the centre of the flour and add most of the milk mix. Stir with a fork, gradually bringing in the flour as you stir. You may not need the rest of the milk, but if the mixture starts to look dry near the end, you can add it then. You should end up with a soft, springy dough. Handling as little as possible, pat the dough into a ball.

Turn out onto a floured surface and flatten the dough gently with your hands no less than 2.5 cm (1") thick. Using a sharp cookie cutter, cut into rounds and place on the baking tray. Knead the scraps and pat out again to cut a couple more scones. Alternatively, to avoid re-rolling, simply pat the dough into a round and cut it into about eight wedges with a sharp knife.

Bake near the top of the oven for 10-15 minutes until risen and golden brown. Remove from the oven and cool on a cooling rack. Serve warm or cold with jam or fruit spread and thick soy cream (p. 167).

Makes 6-8 large scones

1 cup (250 ml) soy milk
1 teaspoon cider vinegar
2 cups (320 g) unbleached flour
2 teaspoons baking powder
½ teaspoon bicarbonate of soda
pinch of salt
4 teaspoons sugar
⅓ cup (65 g) dairy-free spread

Oven 220°C/425°F/Gas 7

chocolate almond fudge shortbread

Look, I know this recipe is way too complicated, not to mention completely over the top with sugar and fat and all. But just try it, once, the way it is written. I promise you it's worth it. Then if you want to feel virtuous next time, bump up the wholemeal flour and miss out the caramel – it's still good, but a little less decadent.

Grease and line the base of a 20 cm x 30 cm (8" x 12") rectangular tin

To make the shortbread, cream the sugar, salt, dairy-free spread and vanilla in a food processor. Sift the flours and add the bran back in. Add the sifted flours to the creamed mixture and pulse to combine. Spread the mixture over the bottom of the tin, using a flat spatula to level off. Bake for 18-22 minutes, until lightly browned. Cool.

For the almond fudge, mix the almond butter, maple syrup and salt in a small bowl. Spread on top of the shortbread. Put the tray in the freezer for 15 minutes.

For the caramel, place all the ingredients in a large, heavy-bottomed pan and heat, stirring constantly, until the sugar dissolves and the mixture starts bubbling madly. Keep at this temperature for 3-5 minutes until it turns a rich caramel colour. Cool a little, then pour on top of the almond fudge layer. Freeze for another 15 minutes.

Melt the chocolate and dairy-free spread or oil in a bain-marie (see p. 27) and cool a little. Pour the chocolate over the toffee layer and roll around to get an even coating. Chill in the fridge for at least an hour, then mark into 12 squares.

Serves 12

SHORTBREAD
¼ cup (50 g) sugar
pinch of salt
½ cup (100 g) dairy-free spread
¼ teaspoon vanilla extract
½ cup (70 g) wholemeal flour
½ cup (80 g) unbleached flour

ALMOND FUDGE LAYER
½ cup (140 g) almond butter
¼ cup (60 ml) maple syrup
¼ teaspoon salt

CARAMEL LAYER
¾ cup (150 g) sugar
¾ cup (150 g) dairy-free spread
½ cup (125 ml) thin soy cream
 (p. 167)
2 tablespoons golden syrup
¼ teaspoon salt

CHOCOLATE TOPPING
1½ bars (150 g) chocolate
1 tablespoon dairy-free spread
 or light oil, e.g. sunflower

Oven 180°C/350°F/Gas 4

chocoblock cookies

Chocoblock full of interesting ingredients including, yes, chocolate chips, but low in fat and sugar and made with wheat-free, wholegrain flours. Best eaten warm from the oven, but will keep for two or three days. Use to make ice-cream sandwiches. Yum.

Grease a large baking tray.

Sift flours, bicarbonate of soda, baking powder, cinnamon and salt into a large bowl. Add oats, coconut, nuts, sultanas and chocolate chips. In a jug or small bowl whisk the oil, vanilla, rice syrup, sugar and date puree. Add the wet to the dry ingredients and mix to a firm dough.

Using a large tablespoon drop balls onto the greased baking tray. Use a large glass or cup dipped in a bowl of water to flatten the cookies a little. Bake for 15-18 minutes until golden brown. Remove from oven, loosen cookies with a metal spatula while still warm and cool on a wire cooling rack.

Makes 12-14

1 cup (140 g) barley flour
1 cup (120 g) oat flour
¼ cup (35 g) brown rice flour
1 teaspoon bicarbonate of soda
¼ teaspoon baking powder
½ teaspoon cinnamon
½ teaspoon salt
½ cup (50 g) rolled oats
½ cup (50 g) desiccated coconut
½ cup (75 g) brazil or other nuts,
   coarsely chopped
½ cup (75 g) sultanas or raisins
½ cup (100 g) chocolate chips
½ cup (125 ml) light oil,
   e.g. sunflower
1 teaspoon vanilla extract
¼ cup (60 ml) rice syrup
¼ cup (50 g) brown sugar
¼ cup (60 g) date puree (p. 39)

Oven 180°C/350°F/Gas 4

bags of energy bars

This recipe is easy to remember – pretty much half a cup of everything. The result is a nutritious, filling, sweet treat. Pack a few in your bag for emergencies.

Put the oats, nuts and seeds in a food processor and blend until chopped. Add the rest of the ingredients and blend until the mixture starts to come together in a ball.

Press into a rectangular shape, about 1 cm (½") thick, on a solid dehydrator sheet. Dehydrate* for 6 hours, then flip and dehydrate for a further 4-6 hours until firm and dry. Cut into bars.

*If you don't have a dehydrator, these can be baked in a greased, lined 23 cm (9") square tin at 150°C/300°F/Gas 2 for 20-25 minutes. They will still be nutritious though not, of course, raw.

Makes 12-16

½ cup (50 g) rolled oats
½ cup (75 g) walnuts, almonds
  or brazils
½ cup (75 g) sunflower seeds
½ cup (75 g) sesame seeds
½ cup (75 g) dried apricots,
  chopped
½ cup (100 g) medjool dates,
  chopped
½ cup (75 g) sultanas
½ cup (50 g) grated apple, about
  1 small apple
1 teaspoon cinnamon
1 teaspoon mixed spice
1 teaspoon vanilla extract
1 teaspoon lemon zest
pinch of salt
¼ cup (60 ml) cold-pressed
  almond, olive or coconut oil

matrimonial cake

I always used to call this dessert 'date slice'. But the original 1930s recipe from Canada is known as matrimonial cake, which I like much better. There are a couple of explanations for the name. One is that the contrast between the rough and smooth textures mirrors the ups and downs of married life; another that two seemingly different sets of ingredients blend together in perfect harmony. As a result matrimonial cake is often served at weddings and bridal showers in the USA and Canada.

Grease and line the base of a 23 cm (9") square tin.

Put the chopped dates in a pan and just cover with orange juice. Bring to the boil and simmer gently until the dates are cooked and the juice is absorbed. Leave to cool.

Sift the flour, bicarbonate of soda, cardamom and salt. Add the oats and sugar. Rub in the dairy-free spread until the mixture becomes like breadcrumbs. Press half the mixture firmly into the tin. Spread the date mixture over the top. Crumble the rest of the oat mixture on top and press down lightly.

Bake for 1 to 1¼ hours until brown on top. Cool in the tin and then cut into 9 squares.

Makes 9

1½ cups (240 g) stoned,
   chopped dates
orange juice
2 cups (280 g) wholemeal flour
½ teaspoon bicarbonate of soda
½ teaspoon ground cardamom
pinch of salt
2 cups (200 g) rolled oats
¾ cup (150 g) sugar
1 cup plus 2 tablespoons (225 g)
   dairy-free spread

Oven 180°C/350°F/Gas 4

chapter three

pies and pastries

I know lots of people who can cook, but say they never make pastry. I think it is a myth that making pastry is difficult. This chapter includes a variety of pastries. I hope that once you've tried a few of them, you'll agree that pastry-making is a cinch. I've tried to include a variety of ingredients and techniques, so that you can see what suits you best.

Baking blind

Recipes often ask you to 'blind bake' the pastry. This means cooking a pastry pie shell before filling. If the pie is going to be cooked with the filling, you only need to part bake the shell, just until the pastry changes colour and starts to lose that 'wet' look. If the filling is to be uncooked, you will need to fully bake the pastry shell. The technique is the same:

● line the pie dish or tin with pastry, allowing a little extra pastry around the edge because it will shrink in the oven

● cut a square of baking parchment and press it into the pastry shell so that the paper extends up the sides

● weigh the paper down with a handful of dry beans or lentils

● bake for the specified time

● remove the beans and paper and bake for a few minutes more to dry out the base

● keep the beans in a jar labelled 'baking beans' to use again next time, and don't try to cook with them!

Pastry guide

De Bolhoed apple pie: rich shortcrust, made with wholemeal flour enriched with almonds and sweetened with rice syrup. A tasty, biscuity, satisfying pastry. This recipe uses some of the pastry mix as a crumble topping, which works well.

Walnut treacle tart: plain shortcrust, made with half wheat and half oat flour. For a shorter (more crumbly) texture, unsweetened. This is a good pastry for lining tart tins but doesn't roll out well so can't be used for pies with lids.

Fruit mince pies: a traditional wholemeal shortcrust pastry, unsweetened. Lighter than some recipes, because of the addition of baking powder and extra liquid. This is a good all-purpose pastry for any type of pie.

Hungarian cheese pie: a light shortcrust, made with unbleached flour, sweetened with a little icing sugar and flavoured with lemon zest. This is a good pastry for carrying a delicate filling, like fruit or custards, when you don't want the pastry to dominate.

Tarte tatin: rich shortcrust, made with wholemeal flour, enriched with almonds and sugar, but lower in fat than most pastry. This has a good flavour and the texture of shortbread, but is fairly robust so needs a good tasty filling to balance it.

Baklava: the only pastry that I've suggested you buy in a shop. I've seen people making filo by hand and, believe me, you don't want to try it. Bought filo pastry is good quality and you get loads in a packet. Well wrapped, it will keep in the fridge for several weeks.

Mini peach pies: a good, all-purpose, gluten-free pastry, made from a mixture of tapioca, besan, rice, quinoa and buckwheat flours. Can be used for any of the recipes in the chapter. Gluten-free pastry is best eaten on the day it is made, so make in small quantities.

Eccles cakes: flaky pastry, made with unbleached white flour and equal amounts of fat and flour (double the fat of shortcrust). Not quite as puffy as puff pastry, but a lot easier to make.

De Bolhoed

It had been a struggle to find vegan food when travelling for three weeks in France and Italy. My two daughters and I had been living, on the whole, on crusty bread and ripe, knobbly tomatoes. The bread and tomatoes in France and Italy are undoubtedly among the best in the world, but one can overdo it. We were desperate to get to Amsterdam and the myriad vegan eats to be had there. De Bolhoed was our destination for brunch on our first morning.

De Bolhoed means 'The Bowler Hat' in Dutch. Contrary to internet rumour it was not built on the site of an old hat shop but started about 25 years ago as a health food store and is now a well-known vegetarian restaurant. The owner just thought the name sounded nice! De Bolhoed sits on the edge of one of Amsterdam's grandest and most beautiful canals, the Prinsengracht, about five minutes walk from the Anne Frank House. You can sit outside by the canal and watch the bikes whizz past,

or choose one of the tables inside the cafe where the walls are decorated with painted pumpkin vines and eclectic artworks. It was busy when we arrived and all the outdoor and window tables were occupied, so we sat at a cosy corner table on bench seats below shelves covered with ornaments. We wondered why a big, fat ginger and white cat was looking at us strangely, but when he leaped up and installed himself in the corner of the bench seat we noticed the indentation in the cushion and the cat hairs that told us this was his place. He deigned to share it with us for the morning.

The food at De Bolhoed is organic, all vegetarian and mostly vegan, with generous portions at a fair price for expensive Amsterdam. The menu is a mix of world cuisines – Mexican, Asian, African, Mediterranean – with an amazing array of salads which are prepared fresh daily. Each day there is a mixed vegan plate on offer, which contains seven or eight different dishes, both hot and cold. And joy of joys, after three weeks of dessert fasting, there was a tall fridge stuffed full of pies, cheesecakes and cakes, many of them vegan.

We had a delicious meal, and although we looked at the other restaurants on my list, we came back to De Bolhoed every day for the rest of our stay in Amsterdam.

De Bolhoed
Prinsengracht 60–62
Amsterdam
Netherlands
Tel: 020 626 1803

De Boelhoed
dutch apple pie

GF* LS

This was our favourite dessert at De Bolhoed, served in gigantic portions with soy cream.

Grease and line the base of a 23 cm (9") round springform tin, with 7 cm (3") sides.

For the filling, put the apples, raisins, lemon zest, liqueur, cinnamon and water in a large pan with a lid and cook over a moderate heat, shaking every now and again, until the apples are soft but not broken up. If there is any liquid at the bottom of the pan remove the lid and raise the heat to boil any excess away. Leave to cool, then fold in the chopped almonds.

For the crust, grind the almonds to fine crumbs in a food processor, then add the flour, salt and lemon zest and blend to combine. Add the vanilla, dairy-free spread and rice syrup and blend until it all comes together in a moist ball. Bring the pastry together with your hands and place in a container in the fridge for 20-30 minutes.

Take three-quarters of the pastry dough and roll out into a circle, about 30 cm (12") across. Lift the pastry into the tin, draping it up the sides of the tin. Don't worry if the pastry breaks, just press it back together using the scraps to fill any gaps. Using your fingers, form a neat top edge. Fill with the apple mixture, pressing it down slightly. Crumble the remaining dough over the top and bake for around 25 minutes until brown. If the pastry starts to get too brown too soon, cover with foil for the remaining baking time. Remove from the oven, stand it on a wire cooling rack and leave to cool in the tin. Remove the outer sleeve of the tin when cool, leaving the base. Serve with soy cream (p. 167), cashew cream (p. 167) or vanilla ice cream (p. 146).

Serves 12

FILLING

1.5 kg (8-10 large) apples, peeled, cored and chopped into 1 cm (½") chunks

⅔ cup (100 g) raisins

1 teaspoon lemon zest

splash of liqueur: Cointreau, Calvados, Amaretto (optional)

2 teaspoons cinnamon

⅔ cup (150 ml) water

½ cup (70 g) almonds, blanched, roasted and chopped coarsely (see p. 15)

CRUST

1 cup (150 g) almonds

2 cups (300 g) wholemeal flour

¼ teaspoon salt

1 teaspoon lemon zest

1 teaspoon vanilla extract

¾ cup (150 g) dairy-free spread

½ cup (125 ml) rice syrup

*or use gluten-free pastry on p. 85

Oven 180°C/350°F/Gas 4

walnut treacle tart

Treacle tart is usually made with sweet, white pastry, white breadcrumbs and bucketloads of golden syrup. This version is healthier and a lot tastier.

You will need a 23 cm (9") loose-bottomed tart tin.

For the pastry, sift the flours and salt. Rub the dairy-free spread into the flour, lightly with just your fingertips, until it resembles breadcrumbs. Sprinkle two tablespoons of the water over the mixture and bring together with a flat knife until it starts to stick together. If it seems too dry, sprinkle more water, little by little, until the pastry comes together and does not seem dry. Then lightly use your hands to bring it together in a ball.

Chill, covered, in the fridge for at least 30 minutes. This pastry is quite crumbly so you can't roll it like conventional pastry. To line the pie dish, cut thin slices of pastry and put them in the dish, side by side, to cover most of the dish. Then use your fingers, or the back of a spoon, to press the pieces together until there are no gaps and the pastry comes right up to the edge of the dish. Trim off any extra pieces and use to fill gaps. Pinch the edges of the pastry so that there is a neat edge, just above the rim of the dish. Bake for 10-15 minutes until the pastry has lost its uncooked look, but is still pale in colour. If you overcook it now, the edges will burn when you bake it with the filling.

For the filling, melt the dairy-free spread, molasses and syrups. Add the other ingredients and combine well. Pour into the pie crust and bake for 20-25 minutes. If the edges look like they are getting too brown, cover them with strips of aluminium foil. Serve warm with vanilla ice cream (p. 146) or soy cream (p. 167).

Serves 12

PASTRY

1 cup (120 g) oat flour
1 cup (140 g) whole-wheat flour
pinch of salt
⅔ cup (130 g) dairy-free spread
2-4 tablespoons cold water
*or use gluten-free pastry on p. 85

FILLING

¼ cup (50 g) dairy-free spread
1 tablespoon molasses
½ cup (125 ml) maple syrup
½ cup (125 ml) golden syrup
¼ cup (60 ml) rice syrup
grated zest of 1 lemon and
    1 orange
1 teaspoon grated fresh ginger
1 cup (100 g) walnuts, chopped
    coarsely
1 apple, skin left on, grated
2 cups (150 g) wholemeal
    breadcrumbs or gluten-free
    crumbs

Oven 180°C/350°F/Gas 4

fruit mince pies

You're bound to want lots of fruit mince come Christmas time, so this recipe makes enough for a few batches of pies. It keeps in the fridge for several months, or you can preserve it in sterilised jars. For me, wholemeal pastry perfectly complements the sweetness of the fruit mince. Because I like the filling more than the pastry, I just put a star on top instead of a lid, but you can put lids on the pies if you prefer.

12-hole shallow tart tin, ungreased.

For the fruit mince, mix all the ingredients in a large bowl and stir thoroughly. Cover and leave the mixture overnight.

Next day, heat the oven to 120°C/225°F/Gas ¼. Place the mincemeat in an ovenproof bowl, seal with foil and allow to cook slowly for 2½ hours. Cool.

For the pastry, sift the flour, baking powder and salt. Put back any bran flakes in the sieve and mix in. Rub in the dairy-free spread, lightly with just your fingertips, until the fat is incorporated and the mixture resembles breadcrumbs. As different wholemeal flours absorb water differently, you'll have to use your judgement as to how much water to add. First, try sprinkling 5 tablespoons onto the flour. Then use your hands to bring the pastry together. If there are dry bits which look like they aren't sticking together, sprinkle a little more water on, until the flour comes easily together into a moist, springy dough. It's better to be a little too sticky at this stage than too dry because the bran will absorb more water as the pastry rests. Cover and chill for half an hour or so before using.

Preheat the oven to 170°C/325°F/Gas 3. Roll out the pastry and cut 12 circles with a 7 cm (3") cookie cutter to line the tart tin. Cut 12 small stars with a star-shaped cutter. Line each depression of the tin, put a big spoonful of fruit mince in the tart and top with a star.

Bake for 10-12 minutes until the pastry is cooked but not browned. Serve warm or cold, with soy cream (p. 167) or cashew cream (p. 167).

Makes 12

FRUIT MINCE

2 medium apples (250 g) peeled, cored and chopped into ½ cm (¼") cubes

⅓ cup (80 ml) light oil, e.g. sunflower

2½ cups (400 g) raisins, sultanas and currants in roughly equal proportions

⅔ cup (100 g) dried apricots, chopped

¾ cup (150 g) brown sugar

zest and juice of 1 orange and 1 large lemon

⅓ cup (50 g) almonds, blanched, roasted and chopped coarsely (see p. 15)

1 tsp ground cinnamon

½ tsp nutmeg

½ tsp ground cardamom

1 teaspoon mixed spice

PASTRY

1½ cups (200 g) wholemeal flour

2 teaspoons baking powder

pinch of salt

½ cup (100 g) dairy-free spread

5-7 tablespoons cold water

*or use gluten-free pastry on p. 85

Oven 170°C/325°F/Gas 3

hungarian cheese pie

I am half-Hungarian, yet to my shame speak only six words of the language (yes, no, little, large, your very good health, sorry). Hungary has a fine culinary heritage but it is very meat and dairy-based. As a child, I grew up with beef goulash, beef stroganoff, paprika chicken and cottage cheese dumplings. I still love the flavour of Hungarian soups and stews, and it's pretty easy to recreate these tastes using beans, vegetables, tofu and tempeh but, until recently, I'd never attempted to recreate my favourite childhood dessert: curd cheese pie, traditionally made with turo, a kind of fresh cottage or curd cheese, mixed with sugar, eggs and sour cream, and topped with meringue. Not the easiest recipe to veganise – but after much experimentation, I now offer a dairy-free version. Sajnálom.

You will need a 23 cm (9") pie dish.

For the pastry, sift the flour with the salt, then rub in the dairy-free spread, lightly with just your fingertips, until the fat is incorporated and the mixture resembles coarse breadcrumbs. Add the sugar and lemon zest and mix in with your fingertips. The idea is to touch this pastry as little as possible to keep it light. Sprinkle 4 tablespoons of water over the crumbs and mix in gently with a flat knife until the crumbs start to stick together. You may need another 1 or 2 tablespoons of water to do this. Lightly roll the pastry into a ball with your hands. You should have quite a moist and soft dough. Place the pastry in the fridge for at least 30 minutes.

Roll out the pastry and place it in the pie dish so that it overhangs the edges of the dish by about 1 cm (½"). Turn the edges under and press your thumb or the handle of a wooden spoon every 1 cm (½") or so all around the rim to make a fluted shape. Blind bake (see p. 68) the pastry shell for about 7-8 minutes, then remove the paper lining and bake for another few minutes to dry out the middle. You don't want the edges to brown at all, or they will burn when you cook the pie with its filling. Remove the pie shell from the oven and cool.

For the filling, mix the soy milk with the lemon juice and leave for a few minutes to thicken. Blend the tofu, cream cheese, icing sugar, lemon zest, cornflour and vanilla extract in a food processor, then add the soy milk mixture and blend again. Pour the filling into the cooled pastry shell and bake for 10-15 minutes, or until the cream cheese mixture is just starting to set.

While it is in the oven, whisk the egg replacer with the water in a bowl big enough to really whisk it properly. You will need a proper whisk; a fork won't do. When the mixture is as fluffy as you can make it, add the icing sugar, a tablespoon at a time, whisking after each addition.

Serves 8

PASTRY

1 cup (160 g) plain white flour

pinch of salt

¼ cup plus 2 tablespoons (75 g) dairy-free spread

¼ cup (35 g) icing sugar, sifted

½ teaspoon lemon zest

4-6 tablespoons cold water

*or use gluten-free pastry on p. 85

FILLING

½ cup (125 ml) soy milk

2 tablespoons lemon juice

1 cup (230 g) silken tofu

1 cup (230 g) vegan cream cheese

⅓ cup (45 g) icing sugar

1 teaspoon lemon zest

3 tablespoons cornflour

1 teaspoon vanilla extract

MERINGUE TOPPING

3 tablespoons egg replacer

6 tablespoons water

¼ cup (35 g) icing sugar, sifted

Oven 180°C/350°F/Gas 4

Remove the pie from the oven and gently spoon on the meringue topping, spreading it carefully over the top all the way up to the pastry edges. Return the pie to the oven, for about another 10 minutes, until the meringue has just set (touch it lightly with your fingers – it still looks wet, so you'll need to feel when it has dried out). To get the characteristic browned look, brush a little light oil or melted dairy-free spread over the top of the meringue and put it under the grill for a minute or two.

Serve warm or cold. *Egészégedre!*

tarte tatin

This recipe was introduced to me by Manu, a lovely French vegetarian chef who worked for me at Bliss Organic Cafe in Adelaide. His pastry is a macrobiotic tart crust, lower in fat and higher in fibre than the puff pastry which is usually used in this recipe. Other than that, it is a traditional French favourite, oozing with sweet, apple-y juices. Be careful when you turn it over as the hot juices can escape!

Ideally, you'll need an ovenproof frying pan or shallow casserole, about 20 cm (8") wide. If you don't have one, grease a similar size cake tin, or ceramic dish.

For the pastry, grind the almonds to fine crumbs in a food processor. Sift the flour, icing sugar and baking powder and add to the bowl. Blend to combine. Add the apple juice and pulse until the mixture resembles coarse crumbs. Add the melted dairy-free spread and pulse again. Pinch the mixture together with your fingers. If it sticks together easily, it is ready. If it crumbles apart, add another tablespoon of apple juice and pulse again, until the mixture comes together into a moist dough. Bring the pastry together with your hands and place in a container in the fridge for 20-30 minutes.

Peel the apples, cut them into quarters and remove the core. Roll the pastry out into a circle and, using your cooking pan as a guide, cut it about 2-3 cm (1") bigger than the pan. Set aside while you make the caramel.

Put the sugar and water in the pan or casserole you will be baking in or, if using a cake tin or ceramic dish, a heavy-based frying pan. Cook over a low heat, without stirring, until the sugar dissolves, then add the dairy-free spread and let it melt. Cook the caramel until it is golden brown. Lay the apples in the caramel, placing them so that the curved side is down – this will be the side you can see when the tarte is turned out. Cook the apples for about 10 minutes, or until they start to turn translucent and brown slightly around the edges.

Remove the pan from the heat and place it on a baking tray or, if you are using a cake tin or ceramic dish, transfer the apples and caramel to this dish, and place on a tray. Lay the pastry on top of the apples, using a spoon to press the pastry gently down over the edge of the fruit. Put the pan and baking tray in the oven and bake for 25-30 minutes, until the pastry is brown. Remove from the oven and leave to settle for 10 minutes. Place a large plate over the top of the pan and, quickly and carefully, invert the whole thing. Be careful as the juices are really hot – use an oven glove to protect your hand. Remove the pan to reveal your tarte tatin. Serve warm or cold with soy cream (p. 167) or vanilla ice cream (p. 146).

Serves 12

PASTRY

⅓ cup (50 g) almonds
1¾ cups (250 g) wholemeal flour
3 tablespoons (25 g) icing sugar
¾ teaspoon baking powder
¼ cup (60 ml) apple juice
⅓ cup (65 g) dairy-free spread, melted
*or use gluten-free pastry on p. 85

CARAMEL

1 cup (200 g) sugar
2 tablespoons water
¼ cup (50 g) dairy-free spread

4-5 apples

Oven 170°C/325°F/Gas 3

baklava

Yes, this is mainly fat and sugar. With more sugar poured on top. But look at all those nuts! Got to be healthier than a cream bun. I have reduced the quantities of sugar and fat a little. But low-fat filo just doesn't work, it looks and tastes like cardboard. So eat just a little.

You will need a 23 cm x 32 cm (9" x 13") baking tin, about 5 cm (2") deep.

For the syrup, heat the sugar, water, agave or maple syrup and cinnamon stick in a heavy-based pan over a medium heat until the sugar dissolves. Then raise the heat and bring the syrup to a boil. Reduce heat and simmer for 10 minutes, then add the lemon zest and juice and allow to cool. Remove cinnamon stick when cool.

For the pastry, melt the dairy-free spread in a small pan. Turn off the heat, but leave the pan on the stove to keep the spread liquid.

The easiest way to deal with the nuts is to grind 1 cup almonds to fine crumbs in the food processor, then put these in a large bowl. Add the other cup of almonds, along with the walnuts and pistachios, to the food processor and pulse until they are coarsely chopped. Mix all the nuts together in the bowl and add the sugar and spices. Stir well to combine.

Count out your sheets of filo pastry and wrap them in a damp tea towel until you are ready to use them to stop them going dry and crispy. Now you can start to assemble the baklava. Remove 6 sheets of filo and cut them with scissors so that they fit the tin. Brush the tin with melted spread, then lay 1 sheet filo in the bottom. Brush again with spread, add another sheet of pastry and repeat until all 6 sheets, plus trimmings, are used up. Take about a third of the nut mixture and sprinkle evenly over the pastry. Then take out another 3 sheets of filo and do the pastry/spread layer thing again. Sprinkle another third of nuts over the pastry, layer another 3 sheets filo, then add the final third of nuts. Finish layering with the remaining 6 sheets of pastry, plus the trimmings, and brush all the remaining spread over the top.

If you are making a gluten-free version of baklava, use a single layer of rolled gluten-free pastry on the bottom of the tin, fill with all the nut mixture and top with another single layer of pastry. You don't need to brush gluten-free pastry with dairy-free spread, as the fat is already in the pastry.

Cut through the top layers of the baklava with a sharp knife. This looks pretty and facilitates serving. You can cut rectangles or diagonally to make diamond shapes.

Bake at 170°C/325°F/Gas 3 for 15 minutes, then reduce the temperature to 120°C/225°F/Gas ¼. Bake for a further 25-30 minutes until golden brown. Remove from the oven and allow to cool in the pan. When completely cold, pour the syrup over the baklava. Refrigerate overnight to allow the syrup to soak in.

Makes about 20 small pieces

SYRUP

1 cup (200 g) sugar

¾ cup (180 ml) water

2 tablespoons agave nectar or maple syrup

1 cinnamon stick

1 teaspoon lemon zest

juice of 1 lemon

PASTRY

¾ cup (150 g) dairy-free spread

1 cup (140 g) almonds, finely ground

1 cup (140 g) almonds, coarsely chopped

1 cup (100 g) walnuts, coarsely chopped

¼ cup (35 g) pistachios, coarsely chopped

½ cup (100 g) flavoursome brown sugar, such as rapadura, sucanat or jaggery (see p. 10)

2 teaspoons cinnamon

1 teaspoon mixed spice

1 teaspoon cardamom

18 sheets filo pastry

*or use gluten-free pastry on p. 85

Oven 170°C/325°F/Gas 3

mini peach pies

These are cute, gluten free and low in sugar. You could use any fruit you like for the filling, or use the pastry to make any of the other recipes in this chapter.

6-hole muffin tin, ungreased.

For the pastry, sift the flour with the salt and sugar, if using. Rub in the fat until the mixture resembles breadcrumbs. Add the water to the flour gradually, mixing with a palette knife or your fingers, until it becomes a workable dough. Cover and chill for an hour or so, but don't leave in the fridge for too long or it could become brittle and crumbly.

For the filling, put the peaches in a pan, with ¼ cup (60 ml) of the water, the star anise and the Amaretto or almond extract, if using, and simmer for a few minutes until the peaches are tender, adding a little more water if necessary. Mix the arrowroot with the rest of the water and add to the pan. Heat until thickened. Add agave or stevia to taste. Cool.

Roll out the pastry and cut six large circles to line the muffin tin and six medium circles for lids. As this is gluten-free pastry, you don't have to worry about over-working the pastry – you can roll and re-roll as many times as you like without fear of the pastry becoming hard and unworkable. Line each hole with a large circle, and fill with the peach mixture. Put a small circle on top and pinch edges together. Prick holes in the top of the pie with a fork, to allow steam to escape. Decorate the pies with leaves cut from the scraps. Brush with the glaze.

Bake for 15-20 minutes until golden. Allow to cool in tin.

Makes 6

PASTRY

1 batch gluten-free flour mix 2 (see box below)
pinch of salt
¼ cup (35 g) icing sugar (optional)
½ cup (100 g) dairy-free spread
3 tablespoons water

FILLING

4 large peaches (about 500 g), chopped into 1 cm (½") cubes
½ cup (125 ml) water
1 piece of star anise
splash of Amaretto, or a few drops of almond extract (optional)
1 teaspoon arrowroot
1 tablespoon agave nectar or a few drops of stevia (see p. 12)

GLAZE

1 teaspoon chickpea (besan) flour, mixed with a little water

Oven 180°C/350°F/Gas 4

Gluten-free flour mix 2 (great for pastry)

¾ cup (100 g) tapioca flour

⅓ cup (50 g) chickpea (besan) flour

¼ cup (35 g) brown rice flour

¼ cup (35 g) quinoa flour

2 tablespoons (20 g) buckwheat flour

Measure all the flour into a big bowl and mix well.

eccles cakes

My daughter tells me that puff pastry, when properly made, is folded 10 times in half and that due to the amazing magic of maths, this results in an incredible 1024 layers in one single thin sheet of puff pastry. Hence mille-feuille *in French and* mille foglie *in Italian, both meaning 'a thousand layers' and referring to a puff pastry slice filled with cream. These little pastries originate in Eccles, a town in Lancashire, England, and are far less pretentious. They are made with an easier version of puff pastry, 'rough puff', which by my reckoning, results in 243 layers, which is good enough for me.*

Grease a baking tray.

Rough puff pastry requires cold hard butter to be gradually integrated into the flour as it is rolled out but most dairy-free spreads are usually soft and spreadable. To overcome this, measure the spread and put it in the freezer overnight.

The next day, sift the flour and salt. Chop the frozen spread into small chunks and add to the flour. Using a flat knife, gently mix the chunks into the flour mixture without breaking them up. Add the water and mix to a firm dough. Bring the pastry together into a ball with your hands, handling it as little as possible. Generously flour the work surface and pat the pastry into a rectangle. Using a well-floured rolling pin, roll the pastry into a strip three times as long as it is wide. Don't worry if the blobs of spread break through – just sprinkle them with flour and carry on rolling. Fold the ends of the strip into the centre so that you have a parcel three layers thick. Press on each end and in the middle with the rolling pin. Turn the pastry through 90° and start the process again: rolling, folding and turning. Do this four times in total. By this time, the spread should have integrated into the flour nicely and the pastry should be light and feel spongy to the touch. Wrap the pastry in greaseproof paper and leave it to rest in the fridge for 20 minutes.

For the filling, melt the spread and mix in the fruit, sugar and zest. Cool.

Roll out the pastry thinly and cut twelve 10 cm (4") circles (use a big mug or a small bowl if you don't have a cutter this size). Put a spoonful of fruit mix in the centre of each circle, leaving a rim around the edge. Gather the edges and pinch them together. Turn the cake over and flatten slightly. Put the cakes on a greased baking tray. Cut 3 slits in each cake with a sharp knife. Brush with the glaze and sprinkle with sugar.

Bake at 220°C/425°F/Gas 7 for 10 minutes, then reduce to 180°C/350°F/Gas 4 for another 5–10 minutes until the pastries are golden brown. Serve warm with custard (p. 168) or soy cream (p. 167). They are also good cold.

Makes 12

ROUGH PUFF PASTRY

1 cup (150 g) unbleached
   white flour

pinch of salt

¾ cup (150 g) dairy-free spread,
   frozen overnight

⅓ cup plus 1 tablespoon (100 ml)
   cold water, with a squeeze
   of lemon

(or use gluten-free pastry on p. 85)

FILLING

2 tablespoons (25 g)
   dairy-free spread

½ cup (80 g) currants

2 tablespoons (25 g) sugar

zest of 1 lemon and 1 orange

GLAZE

1 teaspoon chickpea (besan) or
   soy flour, mixed to a wash with a
   little water

1 tablespoon sugar

Oven 220°C/425°F/Gas 7

chapter four

tarts, trifles and cheese-cakes

This chapter is a bit of a mishmash. You might argue that there is only one actual cheesecake, and even that, being vegan, doesn't contain cheese. I humbly agree. You could say, 'But two of the recipes have pastry – why aren't they in the pies and pastries chapter?' And I would have to answer, 'I don't know.'

I just feel that this selection of desserts belong together. Maybe because they are served cold, maybe because they are particularly creamy and a bit elegant. Or maybe because it's sometimes good to follow your instincts.

Revel Cafe

I first discovered Revel Cafe through a great blog that got my mouth watering with its gorgeous pictures of Revel's vegan cupcakes, and other delicious offerings (aucklandvegan.wordpress.com). Revel does serve an 'omnivorous' menu, but vegans are very well provided for.

I like to start exploring a new city with brunch. This sets me up for a day's sightseeing and saves money by combining two meals. On our first morning in Auckland, my girls and I decided to head for Revel. After an embarrassing few minutes trying to find the location of the unpronounceable Karangahape Road ('K Road' to the locals) we set off. Twenty uphill minutes later, a splash of colour on a rock album-style banner caught my eye – Revel, a cool, retro, higgledy-piggledy place, with nooks and crannies, interesting chairs to try out, toys, board games and, best of all, an old tabletop Space Invaders game.

Our brunch, The Vegan Reveller, included home-made falafel patties, hummus, pesto and relish – a tasty twist on breakfast. We carried out two gorgeous cupcakes to eat later, one pumpkin and chocolate and one lemon. Their cupcake recipes are from *Vegan Cupcakes Take Over the World* (see p. 35). So that's why they're so yummy . . .

Another day and another visit to Revel began with disappointment and ended with joy. Leaving it until late afternoon (this time to indulge in cake, cake, cake) we discovered all the vegan cupcakes sold! Our faces must have looked too sad to bear because the lovely people there quickly offered us a cake that had only just come out of the oven – the vegan chocolate midnight cake. It was delicious.

Revel was started in 2002 with a mission to provide tasty, quality, healthy food, great coffee, friendly and attentive service, with minimal environmental impact. They serve fairtrade organic coffee, use biodegradable takeaway containers and recycle all their food waste.

Revel Cafe
146 Karangahape Rd
Auckland
New Zealand
Tel: 09 309 2372

Revel chocolate midnight cake

This is a magic cake. Depending on how long you cook it, it turns from mousse to cheesecake to cake. The filling could be eaten on its own as a lovely mousse. Cooked for 15-20 minutes, it just sets and cools to a medium-dense cheesecake texture. Cooked a little longer, I am told, it becomes more cake-y. But I love it about halfway between mousse and cheesecake, so I've never gone that far.

Grease and line the base of a 23 cm (9") round springform tin.

For the crust, blend the almonds, sugar, brown rice flour, potato starch and salt in a food processor. When the almonds are finely chopped, add the vanilla and oil and pulse until the mixture becomes like biscuit crumbs. Press into the lined tin and bake for 10 minutes.

For the filling, melt the chocolate in a bain-marie (see p. 27). Blend the tofu, sugar, vanilla and salt in a food processor until very smooth. Add the melted chocolate and blend. Pour the filling onto the base and bake for 15-20 minutes, until the filling is set but jiggles a little. Or longer if you want to test the cake theory.

Cool on a wire rack. When cold, run a palette knife around the edge and release the springform sleeve.

Serves 8

CRUST
½ cup (70 g) almonds
2 tablespoons (25 g) brown sugar
½ cup (70 g) brown rice flour
½ cup (60 g) potato starch
¼ teaspoon salt
1 teaspoon vanilla extract
¼ cup (60 ml) light oil,
  e.g. sunflower

FILLING
2½ bars (250 g) chocolate
1⅔ cup (400 g) silken tofu
¾ cup (150 g) brown sugar
1 teaspoon vanilla extract
¼ teaspoon salt

Oven 180°C/350°F/Gas 4

new york-style lemon cheesecake

I've experimented with many recipes to get the authentic taste and texture of the traditional New York-style cheesecake, a plain, unadulterated baked cheesecake made with cream cheese. Vegan cream cheese is available pretty much everywhere; mixing it half and half with tofu cuts the fat and increases the nutritional value. Don't worry if the cheesecake cracks, this only adds to its authentic look.

Grease a 23 cm (9") round springform tin.

Place a shallow pan filled with water on a lower rack of the oven. This creates a moist atmosphere in the oven that helps create the cheesecake texture.

For the base, sift the flours, baking powder and salt. Put the dairy-free spread and sugar into a food processor and blend together. Add the flour mixture and pulse until incorporated. Flatten into the tin and bake for 10-15 minutes.

For the filling, blend the cream cheese and tofu in a food processor. Add sugar and blend until creamy. Add lemon juice, lemon extract and flour. Blend and pour into crust.

Bake 50-60 minutes until the cheesecake is set, but still wobbles a little when you shake it. Turn off oven but leave the cheesecake in for another half an hour. Remove from the oven and leave the cheesecake to cool completely. Drizzle with the lemon syrup, allowing it to run into any cracks. Run a knife around the edge of the cheesecake and release the springform clip.

Serves 12

BASE
⅓ cup (55 g) unbleached flour
1 cup (140 g) wholemeal flour
1 teaspoon baking powder
¼ teaspoon salt
½ cup (100 g) dairy-free spread
⅓ cup (75 g) brown sugar

FILLING
2 cups (450 g) vegan cream cheese
2½ cups (600 g) silken tofu
⅔ cup (130 g) sugar
½ cup (125 ml) lemon juice
½-1 teaspoon natural lemon extract
   (optional)
⅓ cup (55 g) unbleached flour

TOPPING
1 batch lemon syrup (p. 100)

Oven 180°C/350°F/Gas 4

lime tart

GF R LS

This is such a refreshing summer dessert. Easy to make, and you don't need to turn on the oven in hot weather. The base tastes like a beautiful biscuit crumb; who would know it is just nuts and a few dates? The filling is a creamy pale green, thanks to the avocado, with a zesty flavour that makes your tastebuds tingle. I made this for family friends, who are not really into raw food, and not even vegan. Everyone, including the kids, shouted for more.

You will need four individual tartlet tins, preferably loose-bottomed, or one 23 cm (9") tin.

For the base, place all the ingredients in the food processor and blend, until you can pinch the mixture together and it sticks. If it seems too dry, add one or two more dates. Press firmly into the bottom of the tartlet tins, pushing the mixture well into the fluted edges. Chill for at least an hour.

For the filling, blend all the ingredients except the lime juice and coconut oil in a food processor until very smooth and creamy. Melt the coconut oil by placing it in a glass or ceramic bowl, over another bowl of hot water. Gradually add the lime juice and then the coconut oil, with the motor still running. Pour over the crust and chill in the fridge for at least 3 hours, or in the freezer for an hour.

Sprinkle with lime zest and serve with cashew cream (p. 167)

Makes 4

BASE

1 cup (140 g) brazil nuts

½ cup (50 g) desiccated coconut

⅓ cup (70 g) medjool dates, chopped

FILLING

⅔ cup (90 g) cashews, soaked for 1-2 hours

1 medium avocado (about 120 g flesh)

pinch of salt

seeds of 1 vanilla bean

⅓ cup (80 ml) agave nectar

1 teaspoon lime zest, plus extra for decoration

⅔ cup (160 ml) lime juice, or a mixture of lime and lemon

⅓ cup (80 ml) coconut oil

hello daddy chocolate berry pie

My daughter wanted to make a special treat for her dad when he returned from a long trip. We had recently seen the film Waitress in which the main character invents amazing pies, with long-winded names reflecting major events in her life. Inspired by this, my daughter and I invented this tart and christened it 'hello daddy chocolate berry pie'. Of course, you can pipe whatever message you like on top.

Use a 25 cm (10") glass or ceramic pie dish.

For the pastry, sift the flour and icing sugar into a bowl. Rub the dairy-free spread into the flour, lightly with just your fingertips, until the mixture resembles fine breadcrumbs. Sprinkle over the water and mix with a flat knife, until the pastry starts to stick together. If necessary add another teaspoon or two of water. Using your hands, lightly bring the pastry together into a ball. Cover the pastry and leave in the fridge for at least 30 minutes to rest.

Roll the pastry into a circle approximately 30 cm (12") wide and line the pie dish.

For the filling, wash the berries, chop if large and place in the pastry case. Melt the chocolate in a bain-marie (see p. 27). Whisk the egg replacer with 2 tablespoons soy milk until fluffy, then whisk in the rest of the milk. Blend the tofu, vanilla and agave nectar in a food processor, then add the egg replacer mixture and melted chocolate and blend again until well mixed. Pour over berries.

Bake for 20-25 minutes until set. When cool, pour a layer of soy cream over the top and chill in the freezer for about 30 minutes. Then pipe your message in chocolate ganache.

Serves 8-10

PASTRY

1¼ cups (200 g) white flour
¼ cup (35 g) icing sugar, sifted
½ cup (100 g) dairy-free spread
3 tablespoons (45 ml) water

FILLING

2 heaped cups (250 g) berries of
   your choice
1 cup (150 g) chocolate, chopped
1 tablespoon egg replacer
¾ cup (180 ml) soy milk
1¼ cups (300 g) silken tofu
1 teaspoon vanilla extract
¼ cup (60 ml) agave nectar

ICING (OPTIONAL)

½ cup (125 ml) thick soy cream
   (p. 167)
1 batch chocolate ganache (p. 169)

Oven 180°C/350°F/Gas 4

tiramisu

GF NF

Tiramisu means 'pick me up'. The combination of coffee, chocolate and sugar will certainly do this for you. I usually use decaf coffee to keep my children on this planet.

Grease and line the base of a 30 cm x 20 cm (12" x 8") rectangular tin and grease and line a large flat baking sheet for the cake.

You will need a large, shallow glass or ceramic dish, or 8 individual dessert dishes to assemble the tiramisu.

Bake the vanilla cake mixture in the rectangular tin for about 20 minutes, until risen and golden. Turn out onto a wire cooling rack and cool for 5 or 10 minutes, until it is cool enough to slice into fingers about 4 cm (1½") wide. Lay the fingers sideways on the baking sheet and bake for a further 15 minutes, until they are brown and a little crispy. Place on the rack and allow to cool completely.

Mix the soy cream, cream cheese and icing sugar until smooth, and chill until needed.

Brew the coffee, then dissolve the sugar in it. Allow to cool, then add the liqueur, if using.

Lay the sponge fingers in the base of the large dish (or individual dishes) and pour the coffee mixture over them, saturating them completely. Spoon the cream over the sponge and sprinkle the grated chocolate on top. Chill.

Serves 8

1 batch vanilla cake (basic vanilla, wheat free or gluten free, pp. 43-45)

2 cups (a double batch) thick soy cream (p. 167)

1 cup (220 g) vegan cream cheese

2 tablespoons icing sugar

1 cup (250 ml) double-strength coffee

2 tablespoons sugar

¼ cup (60 ml) coffee liqueur (optional)

⅔ cup (100 g) chocolate, finely grated

Oven 180°C/350°F/Gas 4

lemon raspberry trifle

As a kid I used to love trifle. You know those really big ones, with loads of layers? Packet sponge fingers, packet jelly, tinned fruit salad, packet custard, aerosol squirty cream, hundreds and thousands on top? This version is more to my taste these days – a bit more grown up, and a lot healthier.

You will need a large glass dish.

To make the syrup, put the lemon juice and sugar into a small pan over a low heat until the sugar dissolves. Remove from the heat and leave to cool. Make the cake and custard and leave to cool.

Slice the cake into pieces about 2 cm (1") thick and lay into a glass dish.

Pour the syrup over the cake and leave to absorb while you make the cream.

Scatter the raspberries over the cake. Mix the cream and the cooled custard together and spoon over the top.

Optional – sprinkle with toasted flaked almonds.

Serves 6-8

LEMON SYRUP
½ cup (125 ml) lemon juice
1¼ cups (200g) icing sugar

1 basic vanilla or gluten-free
  sponge, lemon variation, baked
  in a 23 cm (9") square tin
  (p. 43 or 45)
2 punnets fresh or 2 cups (about
  250 g) frozen raspberries
1 cup (250 ml) thick soy cream
  (p. 167)
1 cup (250 ml) thick custard (p. 168)

banoffi tarts

My first job was as a waitress in a great restaurant called The Vineyard, back in my pre-vegan, or even pre-vegetarian days. I loved the food there, and was allowed to taste it all (thank you, Jim, for inspiring my passion for good food and wine!). This was one of my favourite desserts, and I've missed it. So, for this book, I decided to create a dairy-free version. It works! The banana-coffee-toffee combination is sensational. This is best assembled just before you eat it so, if you can, make individual pastry shells beforehand and assemble as you need them – or just eat the whole pie at one sitting!

8 small 12 cm (5") tart tins, or one large 23 cm (9") tin.

For the pastry, sift the flour, icing sugar and salt. Add the lemon zest and vanilla bean seeds, if using. Rub in the dairy-free spread, lightly with just your fingertips, until the fat is incorporated and the mixture resembles coarse breadcrumbs. Sprinkle 3 tablespoons of water over the mixture and mix gently with a flat knife until the crumbs start to stick together. You may need another tablespoon of water to do this. Lightly roll the pastry into a ball with your hands. Cover the pastry and put in the fridge for an hour.

Roll out the pastry and line the tin/s. Prick the base with a fork. Blind bake (p. 68) for 10 minutes then remove the beans and paper and cook for a further 5 minutes until the pastry is lightly coloured around the edges, and you can't see any damp patches. Remove from the oven and cool in the tin.

For the caramel, combine the ingredients in a large saucepan. Heat, stirring constantly, until the sugar dissolves and the mixture turns a light golden brown. Remove from the heat and allow to cool a little. Half fill the pastry cases with caramel.

For the coffee cream, mix the maple syrup, vanilla and coffee with the soy milk in a tall, narrow container that your stick blender will fit into. Insert the blender down to the bottom and switch it on. Keep the blender running, hold your container still and slowly drizzle the oil in, until the cream becomes thick. Chill.

When ready to serve, slice the bananas over the caramel, and spoon the coffee cream on top.

Optional – decorate with grated chocolate and serve with chocolate sauce (p. 170)

Serves 8

PASTRY

1½ cups (240 g) white flour
⅓ cup (50 g) icing sugar
pinch of salt
½ teaspoon lemon zest
seeds of 1 vanilla bean (optional)
⅔ cup (125 g) dairy-free spread
3-4 tablespoons (45-60ml) water

CARAMEL

1 cup (250 ml) soy milk
¾ cup (130 g) dairy-free spread
1¾ cups (350 g) sugar
2 cups (175 g) dried soy milk
1 tablespoon vanilla extract

4-5 large bananas

COFFEE CREAM

1 tablespoon maple syrup
½ teaspoon vanilla extract
2 tablespoons double-strength
  coffee
¼ cup (60 ml) soy milk
⅔ cup (160 ml) light oil,
  e.g. sunflower

Oven 180°C/350°F/Gas 4

chapter five

proper puddings

I'm a pretty tolerant person when it comes to international nomenclature. As a stranger in a strange land, I've had to be. I'll happily ask for zucchini, eggplant and capsicum at the market and snuggle up under my doona at night. I've even been known to talk about my thongs in public!

But I dig my heels in on pudding. Pudding, in general terms, is a not-so-posh way of saying dessert, as in 'What's for pudding, Mum?' More specifically, pudding is a baked or steamed sponge, served with sweet sauce, as in Christmas pudding or sticky date pudding.

The desserts in this chapter are all proper puddings. It should preferably be chilly outside when you eat them, it helps if you have a heap of people round the table and you really have to plan to leave room for them when eating your main course. But you can be sure that when you've eaten them, you are going to feel warmed, nourished and loved.

Some people's idea of a perfect holiday is lying by a pool, novel in one hand, cocktail in the other. Others prefer city sights and a bit of culture. Me, I like tramping up craggy, soggy, misty Cumbrian hillsides with a good breakfast in me and the promise of a warm fire, hot bath and more scrumptious food ahead.

The English Lake District has some spectacular scenery, but the weather can be unpredictable to say the least. So it is essential when you go there to have a place to retreat to when the rain just won't let up. Lancrigg is such a place: roaring fires, squashy sofas, four-poster beds and claw-footed baths. It's an old country house surrounded by acres of woodland, and William Wordsworth and his sister, Dorothy, used to hang out with the original owners. In fact Will probably wrote 'Daffodils' sitting on the terrace, after a roam across the dales.

The food at Lancrigg is organic, vegetarian and all homemade – and vegan or gluten-free diets pose no problem. Breakfasts are gargantuan, just the ticket if you've got a day's walking ahead, or just planning to write poetry in the garden. Traditional English afternoon teas on the lawn or by the fire are everything you'd expect and delicious dinners, served in the elegant candlelit dining room, round off a perfect day of eating.

Lancrigg Vegetarian Country House Hotel

Lancrigg
Grasmere
Cumbria
UK
Tel: 015394 35317

www.lancrigg.co.uk

Lancrigg fig and almond pudding

GF LS

This is a lighter-than-usual baked sponge, gluten free and low in sugar, served with a delicate spiced sauce instead of heavy custard or cream.

Makes 4

TOPPING

2 tablespoons (30 g) dairy-
   free spread
⅓ cup (50 g) almonds, finely
   chopped
⅔ cup (100 g) dried figs, finely
   chopped

SPONGE

⅓ cup plus 1 tablespoon (75 g)
   dairy-free spread
¼ cup (60 ml) maple syrup
½ cup (50 g) soy flour
½ teaspoon baking powder
½ cup (75 g) ground almonds
½ teaspoon vanilla extract
2-4 tablespoons water

SPICED ORANGE SAUCE

¼ cup (60 ml) maple syrup
finely grated zest and juice of
   1 orange
½ cinnamon stick
3 cardamoms, crushed

Oven 150°C/300°F/Gas 2

Grease and line the base of 4 ramekin dishes with baking parchment.

For the topping, mix the dairy-free spread, almonds and chopped figs in a small bowl. Divide the mixture between the ramekin dishes and press down.

For the sponge, cream together the dairy-free spread and maple syrup, either by hand or in a food processor. Sift the soy flour and baking powder and add to the mixture. Stir in the ground almonds and vanilla. Add 2 tablespoons of water or a little more to form a smooth batter. Divide the mixture between the ramekins, covering the fig and almond mixture. Bake for 40-45 minutes, until the puddings are risen and golden.

Remove from the oven and run a knife around the puddings to loosen. Turn out onto a plate.

For the sauce, heat the maple syrup, orange zest, juice and spices in a pan and simmer for a few minutes. Remove the spices and spoon the sauce around the puddings.

sticky date puddings with toffee sauce

Sticky date pudding is a great Australian favourite. The sponge in this vegan version is a little less sweet than many recipes, but the sauce is the full whack!

Grease 6-8 individual pudding tins or large muffin tins. These puddings can stick, so it's a good idea to cut a small circle of baking parchment to sit in the base of each tin.

For the pudding, soak the dates in the coffee and boiling water and leave while you assemble the other ingredients.

Sift the flour, baking powder, bicarbonate of soda and spices into a medium bowl. In a smaller bowl, mix the soy milk and vinegar, leave to thicken for a few minutes, then add the vanilla extract, oil and sugar.

Add the soy milk mixture and the soaked dates to the flour and mix well.

Pour the batter into the greased tins, about three-quarters full. Bake for 20-25 minutes until the puddings have risen and spring back when you press them slightly. Remove from the oven, cool for around 5 minutes, then slide a palette knife around each pudding and turn out carefully.

For the toffee sauce, combine all the ingredients in a pan and place over a low heat, without stirring, until the sugar has melted. Then stir with a wooden spoon to combine the ingredients and simmer for about 5 minutes.

Serve the puddings, warm, slathered with toffee sauce and vanilla ice cream (p. 146).

Serves 6-8

PUDDING

1 cup (160 g) dates, stoned and chopped small

2 tablespoons double-strength coffee

½ cup (125 ml) boiling water

1¼ cups (200 g) unbleached flour

1 teaspoon baking powder

¾ teaspoon bicarbonate of soda

¼ teaspoon cinnamon

¼ teaspoon ground ginger

½ cup soy milk

1 teaspoon cider vinegar

1 teaspoon vanilla extract

⅓ cup (80 ml) light oil, e.g. sunflower

¾ cup (150 g) sugar

TOFFEE SAUCE

½ cup (125 ml) thin soy cream (p. 167)

1 cup (200 g) brown sugar

½ cup (100 g) dairy-free spread

½ teaspoon vanilla extract

pinch of salt

Oven 180°C/350°F/Gas 4

bread pudding

I grew up on this old English favourite. Like bread and butter pudding (p. 119), it was originally invented as a cheap pudding to use up stale bread. Unfortunately, modern bread is so loaded with preservatives that it tends to go mouldy before it dries out, and if you make your own, without preservatives, people are so delighted they eat it all before it gets a chance to go stale. Try catching end-of-the-day offers on artisan bread in a good baker or health food store, or make your own and hide it for a few days!

Grease and line a 23 cm (9") square tin or ceramic dish.

Cut or tear the bread into small chunks and place in a large bowl with the sultanas, prunes and apricots. Cover with the soy milk and soak for 20 minutes.

Add the rest of the ingredients and beat well, so that the bread breaks down a bit and everything is well combined.

Press into the tin and bake for around an hour until firm and brown. You can eat this warm from the oven, but it tastes even better the next day. Serve as it is or with soy cream (p. 167), custard (p. 168) or vanilla ice cream (p. 146).

Serves 8

450 g (1 lb) stale wholemeal bread, without crusts

1 cup (160 g) sultanas

½ cup (75 g) ready-to-eat prunes, chopped

½ cup (75 g) ready-to-eat dried apricots, chopped

2½ cups (625 ml) soy milk

½ cup (100 g) dairy-free spread, melted

¾ cup (150 g) dark brown sugar

450 g (1 lb) apples, peeled, cored and chopped

egg replacer to equal 2 eggs

zest and juice of 1 orange

2 teaspoons cinnamon

2 teaspoons mixed spice

¼ teaspoon nutmeg

Oven 180°C/350°F/Gas 4

coconut rice pudding

This nutritious update on a nursery favourite should please all kids and all those who remember being a kid.

Grease a medium glass or ceramic baking dish.

Measure all the ingredients, except the pistachio nuts, into a large bowl and stir to mix. Pour the mixture into the baking dish and cover with a lid or foil. Place the dish on a baking tray, to catch any drips, and place on the bottom shelf of the oven. After 30 minutes carefully remove the tray, stir the rice and place back in the oven. Set the timer for another 30 minutes, stir again and check to see if the rice is soft – if it is not, return to the oven for another 15 minutes. If at any stage you think the pudding is getting too dry, add a little more rice or soy milk and stir in. Serve warm or cold, sprinkled with chopped pistachio nuts.

Serves 6

PUDDING

¾ cup (125 g) risotto (arborio) rice

⅓ cup (50 g) sultanas or raisins

½ cup (50 g) grated apple, about 1 small apple

¼ cup (60 ml) agave nectar or maple syrup

1 teaspoon vanilla extract

½ teaspoon cinnamon

¼ teaspoon nutmeg

1 tin (400 ml) coconut milk

1 cup (250 ml) rice or soy milk

TO SERVE

1 tablespoon unsalted pistachio nuts, chopped

Oven 170°C/325°F/Gas 3

plum and pecan crumble

Whoever invented crumbles deserves a medal for creating one of the easiest and most popular desserts ever. Chop up any fruit in the house, rub a bit of fat into some flour and stir in some sugar, throw it on top of the fruit, whack the whole lot in the oven and away you go – a fantastic, warming winter sweet, needing only a good dollop of custard or ice cream to complete it perfectly. This crumble adds a couple more refinements to justify it being in a recipe book.

You will need a shallow 1 litre (2 pint) glass or ceramic baking dish.

Halve the plums and layer them in the dish, packing them tightly together. Sprinkle with one to two tablespoons of the brown sugar, reserving the other tablespoon to sprinkle on top of the crumble. Bake the plums for about 15 minutes in the oven, until they start to soften.

Meanwhile, measure the barley flour into a large bowl and using your fingertips rub the dairy-free spread into the flour, until the mixture looks like lumpy breadcrumbs. Stir in the sugar, rolled oats and pecans.

When the plums come out of the oven, spoon the crumble on top and press down around the fruit. Sprinkle the remaining tablespoon of brown sugar over the surface if you like a crunchy, sweet top (omit for *LS*). Bake for 30-40 minutes until the crumble looks crunchy and lightly browned. Serve with custard (p. 168) or vanilla ice cream (p. 146).

Serves 8

10-12 large (750 g) plums
2-3 tablespoons (25 g) brown sugar
1 cup (140 g) barley flour
⅓ cup (65 g) dairy-free spread
¼ cup (50 g) sugar
½ cup (50 g) rolled oats
½ cup (50 g) pecans, roughly chopped

Oven 200°C/400°F/Gas 6

apple and blackberry betty

NF

Unlike a charlotte, which consists of layered slices of sugared bread with fruit in the middle, a betty is fruit topped with a layer of breadcrumbs and sugar. Many people confuse the two. My grandmother was a Charlotte, and I could have been a Betty (short for my full name, Elisabeth), so I feel a responsibility to clarify this matter.

You will need a 1 litre (2 pint) shallow glass or ceramic baking dish.

Melt the dairy-free spread in a frying pan over a low heat. Once melted add the sugar, syrup, lemon zest and juice and stir until dissolved. Add the breadcrumbs and stir until they soak up all the liquid. Remove from the heat and mix in the ground hazelnuts, if using.

Layer the apples in the bottom of the dish and scatter the blackberries on top. Sprinkle the crumb mixture on top and bake for 20-25 minutes, or until the fruit is soft and the crumbs are lightly browned. Serve warm with soy cream (p. 167) or cashew cream (p. 167).

Serves 6

¼ cup (50 g) dairy-free spread

⅓ cup (65 g) brown sugar

2 tablespoons golden syrup

zest and juice of ½ lemon

2 large slices (125 g) wholemeal
   bread, broken into breadcrumbs

2 tablespoons (25 g) ground
   hazelnuts (omit for NF)

3-4 (500 g) large apples, peeled,
   cored and thinly sliced

1 cup (125 g) blackberries

Oven 180°C/350°F/Gas 4

berry cobbler

If possible, this is even easier than a crumble. Any kind of fruit can be used as the base. Berries are lovely because of the bright colours and all those antioxidants! I used blackberries, blackcurrants and blueberries, but any mixture of berries would do – just try and have a mixture of sweet and tart. The topping is simply stirred together and then plopped on top, leaving gaps for the fruit to ooze through. The result looks like cobblestones, hence the name. I've seen some neat and tidy versions where a scone (biscuit) dough is made and cut into circles and laid on top, but honestly, who wants to do that when you can have the fun of throwing lumps of dough around?

Grease a glass or ceramic baking dish, about 20 cm x 20 cm (8" x 8") or 6 individual ramekin dishes.

For the filling, mix the berries, sugar and arrowroot and place in the baking dish or ramekins.

For the topping, stir the lemon juice and zest into the soy milk and leave for a few minutes to thicken. Then add the oil and whisk together. Sift the flour, baking powder, salt and cinnamon, then stir in the sugar. Mix the milk and flour into a sticky dough. Now 'cobble' – drop spoonfuls of the dough randomly all over the top of the berries, leaving gaps between.

Bake for 25-30 minutes until the dough has risen and browned and the berries are bubbling through the gaps. Serve warm with soy cream (p. 167) or vanilla ice cream (p. 146).

Serves 6

FRUIT FILLING

3 cups (about 450 g) mixed berries

⅓ cup (65 g) sugar

2 tablespoons arrowroot

TOPPING

1 teaspoon lemon juice

1 teaspoon lemon zest

¾ cup (180 ml) soy milk

¼ cup (60 ml) light oil,
    e.g. sunflower

1½ cups (240 g) unbleached flour

2 teaspoons baking powder

¼ teaspoon salt

½ teaspoon cinnamon

3 tablespoons sugar

Oven 180°C/350°F/Gas 4

bread and butter pudding

LS NF

This one takes me back to my childhood. I can remember peering through the door of the oven, looking to see if the top was brown enough. My favourite part was the crispy top layer, so it was important to wait for just the right amount of brown-ness.

Grease a glass or ceramic baking dish, about 20 cm x 20 cm (8" x 8").

Spread each slice of bread thickly with dairy-free spread, reserving a little spread for the top. Cut each slice into four triangles. Place a layer of bread slices, spread side up, in the bottom of the dish, cutting pieces to fit in the gaps. Sprinkle with a tablespoon of sugar and about half the raisins or sultanas. Cover with another layer of bread, another tablespoon of sugar and the rest of the dried fruit. Finish with a layer of bread, overlapping the slices so that the points of the triangles stick up a little – these corners should turn brown and crispy.

Mix the chickpea flour and cornflour in a large jug or bowl. Gradually whisk in the milk. Pour the mixture evenly over the bread slices. Put in the fridge for 30 minutes to an hour to allow the bread to soak up some of the liquid.

Sprinkle the rest of the sugar on top of the pudding and dot with the remaining dairy-free spread. Bake for 30-35 minutes, until crisp and golden brown. My mum used to fob me off with more milk poured on top, but I recommend trying it with thin soy cream (p. 167).

Serves 6-8

250-300 g good white bread, sliced
    thinly (about 6-8 slices)
¼ cup (50 g) dairy-free spread
¼ cup (50 g) sugar
½ cup (80 g) raisins or sultanas
¼ cup (70 g) chickpea (besan) flour
2 tablespoons cornflour
2 cups (500 ml) oat, rice or soy milk

Oven 180°C/350°F/Gas 4

lemon syrup sponge pudding

Who doesn't remember syrup sponge? There was never enough syrup, was there? This version has lots, but with the addition of lemon to cut the sweetness a little and make it go further.

Grease a 1 litre (2 pint) pudding basin with dairy-free spread.

Pour the golden syrup into the base of the pudding basin. Stir in half the lemon juice.

Sift the flours, baking powder, bicarbonate of soda and salt. In a separate bowl or jug, whisk the rest of the lemon juice and the zest into the soy milk and leave for a few minutes to thicken slightly. Add the oil and sugar to the milk mixture and whisk together. Add the wet ingredients to the flour mixture and stir until combined. Pour the sponge mixture into the basin.

Cover the basin with baking parchment (leaving a pleat to allow for expansion) and tie with string. Place the bowl in the top section of a steamer and steam for 1½ hours. If you don't have a steamer use a large pan with a lid, and a trivet or upturned saucer in the bottom for the pudding basin to sit on. Keep an eye on the water level throughout the cooking time and top up with boiling water when necessary.

When the time is up, carefully remove the pudding from the steamer and remove the paper. Check the pudding is cooked by inserting a skewer – if it comes out dry it is done. Leave to settle for about 5 minutes, then run a palette knife around the edge and turn the pudding onto a large plate.

Serve with custard (p 168).

Serves 8-10

½ cup (200 g) golden syrup
juice of 1 lemon
¾ cup (120 g) unbleached
   white flour
½ cup (70 g) wholemeal flour
1 teaspoon baking powder
½ teaspoon bicarbonate of soda
¼ teaspoon salt
1 teaspoon lemon zest
1 cup (250 ml) soy milk
⅓ cup (80 ml) light oil,
   e.g. sunflower
½ cup (100 g) sugar

christmas pudding

GF LS NF

This recipe was based on my mum's, which was based on her mum's, and I expect my daughters will carry on the tradition – each generation altering the recipe a little, adding its own tidbit of history. My mum used to make her pudding weeks before Christmas but, even though I intend to every year, I never seem to manage it. It still tastes good, even if it hasn't had time to mature properly. It's traditional in our family that everyone gives the pudding mixture a stir and makes a wish. But I've abandoned my mum's habit of wrapping a coin in foil and hiding it in the pudding, because of my anxiety about choking or aluminium poisoning!

Grease a 1 litre (2 pint) pudding basin.

Mix the dried fruit, grated apple, lemon and orange zest and spices in a large bowl. Pour over the beer, orange and lemon juice, and brandy or rum, stir well, cover and leave overnight.

Next morning sift the flour and baking powder and add to the fruit mixture, along with the breadcrumbs, sugar and salt. Mix the molasses with the oil and stir into the mixture. Now everyone have a stir and make a wish.

Pack the mixture into the pudding basin and flatten the surface. Cover the basin with a double layer of baking parchment and a layer of foil (leaving a pleat to allow for expansion) and tie with string.

Place the bowl in the top section of a steamer and steam for 6 hours. If you don't have a steamer, use a large pan with a lid, and a trivet or upturned saucer in the bottom for the pudding basin to sit on. Keep an eye on the water level every 1 to 2 hours throughout the cooking time and top up with boiling water when necessary.

When the time is up, carefully remove the pudding from the steamer and allow to cool in the bowl. Then remove the parchment and foil, and cover the basin with new parchment and foil. Keep in a cool, dark place or, in a warm climate, the fridge, until Christmas. To reheat, steam for 1 to 2 hours. Serve with custard (p. 168) or vanilla ice cream (p. 146).

Serves 12

5 cups (800 g) mixed dried fruit,
 e.g. sultanas, raisins, currants,
 chopped figs, chopped prunes,
 candied peel, sour cherries,
 or similar
1 large apple, grated
juice and zest of 1 lemon and
 1 orange
1 teaspoon nutmeg
1 teaspoon cinnamon
1 teaspoon mixed spice
½ cup (125 ml) beer
2 tablespoons brandy or rum
 (optional)
1 cup (140 g) wholemeal flour or
 gluten-free flour mix 1 (p. 45)
2 teaspoons baking powder
2 cups (125 g) breadcrumbs
 (or gluten-free breadcrumbs)
½ cup (100 g) dark brown sugar
¼ teaspoon salt
2 tablespoons molasses
¾ cup (180 ml) light oil,
 e.g. sunflower

chapter six
fruit
desserts

If we are 98 per cent genetically similar to apes, we probably ought to live on a diet based mainly on fruit. Nutrient-rich, with the sweetness we all seem to crave, fruit can provide a complete diet, especially if the vegetable-fruits (avocadoes, tomatoes, sweet peppers, cucumbers) are included. I love to eat only fruit at breakfast time, either one single variety, or a fruit salad or mixed fruit juice. It's sweet, cleansing and provides instant energy – better than a shot of caffeine to get you going in the morning.

Fruit also makes a great dessert, with most of the sweetness coming from the natural sugars in the fruit rather than added sugars. Cooking fruit often makes it palatable to people who profess not to like fruit, although many of the nutrients are lost this way.

The raw food revolution is happening! Radiant, happy people all over the world are telling us of the benefits of a raw food diet, and they look so great it's easy to believe them. 'Raw' means unprocessed, often organic food in its natural state. Any heating is below 40-46 °C (104-115 °F), the temperature at which the enzymes in food are destroyed. A raw food diet is naturally gluten free, low in sugar and usually vegan. It doesn't contain artificial additives like flavours, colours or preservatives. Instead, it is full of vitamins and bursting with antioxidants. Raw foodists say they get loads of energy from this diet which, they argue, is the best defence against premature ageing and disease. You don't have to restrict yourself only to raw foods to enjoy the benefits, just incorporate more raw food such as fruit, freshly squeezed vegetable juices, green smoothies, raw muesli, salads, dried fruits and nuts into your diet. If you get enthusiastic, gourmet raw food preparation will leave your tastebuds tingling. Not sure how good it will taste? Start with some of the dessert recipes in this book such as lime tart, black forest gateau or chocolate chunk ice cream (p. 95, 40 and 153) and you'll be convinced.

I was very excited when I heard that a raw food restaurant had opened in Melbourne, le cru – which means 'raw' in French. Carolyn Trewin, the founder of le cru, told me she became convinced of the benefits of raw food through her experience of breast cancer. Trying to find answers, she studied cell rejuvenation and the treatment of tumours with a living wholefood alkaline diet for four years. Her daughter, Nush, the chef, prepares 'Living Cuisine' with passion, love and commitment – blending, sprouting, fermenting and dehydrating vegetables, fruits, nuts, seeds, sea vegetables, Irish Moss, fresh herbs and exotic spices.

I started an incredible meal with beetroot ravioli and smoky lapsang mushrooms, followed by potato salad and ruby kraut. For dessert, my friend and I shared a pineapple carpaccio and a slice of chocolate ganache cake with coconut cream. And we drank a lovely organic New Zealand riesling – wine is raw after all! The food was beautiful to look at, colourful and flavoursome – a delight to every sense.

Carolyn and Nush are now concentrating on developing their wholefoods business, supplying delicious raw, vegan ice cream, crackers and granola to the retail and catering industry. Sadly for raw food fans, the restaurant is now closed, but you can buy many of Nushie's Natural products in stores and online.

www.nushiesnatural.com.au

le cru pineapple carpaccio

GF R

This is a refreshing, summery dessert easy enough for anyone to make.

Serves 8

CARPACCIO

1 small pineapple

2 tablespoons rum or
   pineapple juice

¼ cup (60 ml) agave nectar

SORBET

1 large pineapple, chopped

¾ cup (180 ml) agave nectar

⅛ teaspoon ground cardamom

For the carpaccio, slice the pineapple very finely with a sharp knife or mandolin. Soak the slices in the rum or pineapple juice and agave nectar overnight.

Choose 8 perfect slices and reserve for garnish. If you have a dehydrator, you can dry these for 8 hours to make beautiful pineapple crisps.

For the sorbet, blend all the ingredients in a food processor or blender until smooth and freeze according to your ice-cream maker's instructions. Alternatively, follow instructions on p. 141 for freezing without an ice-cream maker.

To serve, place slices of pineapple onto a plate in a circle. Place a scoop of sorbet in the centre and top with a pineapple slice or crisp.

winter fruit compote

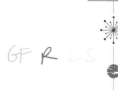

GF R LS

This is a great winter dessert, served with plain soy yogurt or raw cashew cream (p. 167). I love it on porridge in the morning, too, for a breakfast you can't fault: full of fibre, jam-packed with vitamins and minerals and it'll keep you glowing all the way until lunchtime . . .

Squeeze the orange and pour the juice into a dish with about the same amount of water. Add the fruit and spices, making sure they are submerged, and leave overnight. Remove the spices before serving.

Serves 2-3

8 dried apricots

8 prunes

a handful of sultanas

a sprinkling of goji berries

juice of 1 orange

1 stick of cinnamon

2 cloves

a small piece of star anise

amaretto peacherines

GF LS

I love peacherines. I had never heard of them until I moved to Australia, so I'm not sure if they are available in the rest of the world. They are a cross between a peach and nectarine, as I'm sure you have guessed, combining the best of both. They are large, smooth-skinned, fleshy and juicy. If you can't get them, use the biggest nectarines you can find. This is a very simple summer dessert, made special by the addition of Amaretto. If you haven't got it, or want the dessert to be alcohol free, just add a drop of almond extract to the agave and spread mixture. You can also char-grill these on a barbecue or griddle.

Melt the dairy-free spread and mix in the agave nectar and Amaretto or almond extract. Cut the peacherines or nectarines in half and place cut side up on a baking tray. Brush the Amaretto mixture on the fruit.

Put the tray under the grill for 8-10 minutes. Serve with cream or ice cream and drizzle the remainder of the syrup on top.

Serves 6

2 tablespoons (25 g) dairy-free
   spread
2 tablespoons (30 ml) Amaretto (or
   1-2 drops almond extract)
2 tablespoons (30 ml) agave nectar
6 peacherines or nectarines

vanilla-poached pears with hazelnut-fig filling

GF LS

My favourite dessert as a child was Poire Belle Helene. My mother always knew how to posh things up, even when it was a tin of pears and bought ice cream. She did, however, always make home-made chocolate sauce. I remember she put ground almonds in the sauce – always trying to sneak the healthy things in where I wouldn't notice them.

This grown-up version has the nuts hidden inside the pear instead, which is filled with a mixture of roasted hazelnuts, figs and goji berries, with a hint of orange. You can serve the pears with a reduction of the poaching syrup, for a low sugar option, but they are still best with vanilla ice cream and chocolate sauce!

Peel the pears, leaving the stalk, and place upright in a saucepan just big enough to hold them. Add the agave nectar, cinnamon, whole vanilla bean, star anise and enough water to just cover the pears. Cover and bring to a simmer over a medium heat. Poach the pears for 15-20 minutes until a skewer goes in easily. Remove the pears carefully and place in a dish in the fridge to cool. Remove the whole spices and carry on simmering the liquid until it has reduced to a thickish syrup. Remove from the heat, transfer to a heatproof container and allow to cool.

For the filling, blend the hazelnuts, figs and orange zest in a food processor until finely chopped. Strain the goji berries or sultanas and stir them in, along with enough orange juice to make the mixture stick together.

To stuff the pears, cut a thin slice off the bottom of each pear to leave a flat surface so that it will stand up. Using a narrow, sharp knife, carefully cut a circle around the core of the pear and hollow out with a spoon. Fill each pear with as much of the hazelnut mixture as you can and stand it upright in a serving dish. Drizzle the pears with the reduced poaching syrup.

Serve cold, with ice cream and chocolate sauce if desired.

Serves 6

PEARS

6 large, firm pears
¼ cup (60 ml) agave nectar
1 cinnamon stick
1 vanilla bean, split
1 star anise
1-1½ cups (250-375 ml) water

FILLING

⅓ cup hazelnuts, roasted and
   skinned (see p. 15)
3-4 (80 g) dried figs, chopped
1 teaspoon orange zest
2 tablespoons goji berries or
   sultanas, soaked in hot water
1-2 teaspoons orange juice

OPTIONAL, TO SERVE

vanilla ice cream (p. 146)
easy chocolate sauce (p. 170)

apple and strawberry jelly

GF LS

My friend Jenni made these for her son's birthday party, but they were so tasty that all the adults wanted to eat them.

You will need 6 small glasses or glass dessert dishes.

Sprinkle the agar powder onto the apple juice in a large pan and leave to soak for 15 minutes. Place over a medium heat and bring to the boil. Simmer for 15 minutes. Don't worry if the mixture doesn't look thick, it will thicken on cooling. Don't add more agar powder than suggested, otherwise you will have rock-like jellies.

Keep an eye on the mixture as it cools and when it begins to thicken, fill the glasses one third full with jelly. Add a layer of strawberries and sprinkle with a teaspoonful of hazelnuts. Add another layer of jelly, strawberries and nuts, then finish with a jelly layer. Leave to set completely in the fridge. To serve, top with a drizzle of maple syrup and a strawberry.

Serves 6

2 teaspoons agar powder

1 litre clear apple juice

½ cup (70 g) hazelnuts, roasted, skinned and ground (p. 15)

1 cup (150 g) strawberries, sliced

2 tablespoons maple syrup

five grain pancakes with flambeed bananas

This is a basic pancake recipe that you can adapt to suit any occasion. The recipe suggests five different flours, which makes a nutritious, low-gluten, high-fibre pancake. However, you can use any variety of flour you like, as long as the total amount of flour adds up to three cups (about 400 g). You can also choose which milk you like – soy, rice, oat or nut. You can make thick American-style pancakes, using a little less liquid, or thinner crepes, using a little more. You can use the pancakes for sweet or savoury dishes. A very versatile recipe!

This version makes a great winter dessert. Setting fire to your food is always fun and impresses big and little kids.

Sift the flours, baking powder and salt together and add any bran or coarse bits back in. Pour the milk into a blender, add half the flour mixture and blend. Add the rest of the flour and blend until smooth. Pancake batter improves if you leave it to stand for about 30 minutes. Heat a good non-stick or cast iron pan over a medium heat. Add a splash of oil and roll the pan around to cover the base. If the oil starts to smoke, the pan is too hot. If it doesn't roll around the pan easily, the pan is not hot enough. You don't want too much oil, only enough to just coat the base of the pan. If you pour too much in by mistake, empty it into a heatproof bowl and use it for the other pancakes. Pour about ¼-⅓ cup (4-5 tablespoons) batter into the pan and roll around to spread out a little. This mixture is half way between a crepe and an American pancake. If you want a thinner crepe, add a little more milk to the batter. If you want American-style pancakes, use a little less milk and don't roll the pan, just allow the mixture to settle by itself. Allow the pancake to cook until the surface dries out. This should take about 45 seconds to one minute. Using a flat spatula, ease the pancake over and cook the other side. If you find that the pancake is a bit too brown when you turn it over, turn the heat down a bit. If it takes more than a minute for the pancake to dry out, turn the heat up a bit. Once you've got the correct heat, repeat the process for all the other pancakes, greasing the pan with just a bit of oil each time. Keep the pancakes warm in a low oven while you're cooking the rest.

Cut the bananas in thick diagonal slices. Melt the dairy-free spread in a large frying pan and fry the banana slices, until they start to brown. Add the sugar and allow it to melt. Add the rum and quickly touch a match to it. Allow the flames to burn out naturally.

To serve, place a few slices of banana in the centre of a crepe and roll up. Good with soy cream (p. 167), peanut butter ice cream (p. 145) or praline ice cream (p. 149).

Serves 6

PANCAKES

⅓ cup (50 g) buckwheat flour
⅔ cup (90 g) maize flour
1 cup (120 g) oat flour
½ cup (70 g) barley flour
½ cup (70 g) spelt flour
2 teaspoons baking powder
pinch of salt
1 litre soy, rice, oat or nut milk
light oil, e.g. sunflower, for frying

BANANAS

6 large bananas
¼ cup (50 g) dairy-free spread
2 tablespoons brown sugar
3 tablespoons rum

summer pudding

Summer pudding is a traditional English dessert which combines a mixture of summer fruits with bread. It was invented in the 19th century, when it was known by the delightful name of 'hydropathic pudding' because it was served in health spas, as a healthier alternative to pastries. Fortunately, someone in the early 20th century thought of the name 'summer pudding' and the recipe survives to this day. It has a beautiful ruby red colour and intense fruit flavour, without the heaviness of a pie or crumble. Raspberries and redcurrants are the best fruits to use, but you can also add small amounts of blackberries, black cherries and blackcurrants. Traditionally white bread is used, to show the rich red colour, but you could use a very light wholemeal. I haven't tried it with gluten-free bread, but I don't see why it wouldn't work.

You will need a 1 litre (2 pint) pudding basin, and a saucer that just fits inside the rim of the basin.

If the fruits are fresh, wash and remove any stalks or stones. Put the fruit, sugar and water in a large, heavy-based pan over a low heat, until the sugar dissolves and the juices begin to run – about 3 or 4 minutes for fresh fruit; 9 or 10 minutes for frozen.

Line the pudding basin with the slices of bread, tearing them to fit and overlapping slightly. Save some of the bread to cover the pudding.

Strain the fruit and save about half a cup (125 ml) of the juice in a separate container. Spoon the fruit and remaining juice into the bread-lined basin. Cover the surface of the fruit with the remaining bread, cover with the saucer and place a heavy weight on top (a few cans of baked beans or similar work well). Chill overnight in the fridge.

To serve, remove the saucer, place a serving dish upside-down over the basin and invert quickly. Unmould the pudding, spoon the remaining juice over any parts where the white of the bread is still showing, and serve with chilled soy or cashew cream (p. 167).

Serves 6

3 cups (750 g) mixed summer soft
  fruits (raspberries, redcurrants,
  blackberries, black cherries or
  blackcurrants), fresh or frozen
½ cup (100 g) sugar
3 tablespoons (45 ml) water
6-8 slices (about 250 g) white, light
  wholemeal or gluten-free bread,
  crusts removed

baked apples

Why, oh why, can't I buy Bramley apples in Australia? I fantasise about their melting puffiness when baked or stewed, and grit my teeth over the firmness of the apples I am trying to cook. If you can get Bramleys for this recipe, I envy you. If not, Granny Smiths are the best alternative.

You will need an ovenproof dish big enough to hold the apples.

Mix all the filling ingredients in a small bowl and leave for about 30 minutes, so that the dried fruit soaks up the juice.

Wash and core the apples, digging away quite a big hole, so that you can fit in lots of filling. Cut a horizontal slit just through the skin around the centre of each apple. If you don't do this, there could be an explosion in your oven which is not nice to clean up. Stuff as much filling as you can into each apple and sit them upright in the dish. Sprinkle 4 tablespoons water around the apples and cover the dish with a lid or foil.

Bake for 45 minutes to an hour, until the apples are soft. Serve warm with custard (p. 168).

Serves 4

4 of the largest apples you can find

FILLING

½ cup (70 g) sultanas or raisins

4 (about 60 g) medjool dates, finely chopped

¼ cup (35 g) ready-to-eat prunes, finely chopped

2 tablespoons almonds, chopped (omit for NF)

½ teaspoon cinnamon

juice of one orange

Oven 200°C/400°F/Gas 6

chapter seven

ice creams and sorbets

Okay, so there are some places on the planet where you can buy yummy, reasonably healthy vegan ice cream. Adelaide, South Australia, is not one of them. When I moved here, an occasional tinkering with home-made ice cream became a serious, full-time occupation.

I tried lots of recipes for vanilla ice cream, but found many of them too watery or too beany (though I love tofu, in my opinion it has no place in ice cream). I decided to imitate conventional dairy recipes, using soy cream instead of double cream, but this tasted too fatty. In the end, the perfect combination was half custard and half cream; thick and creamy with just enough fat, but not too much. My basic vanilla is a big hit with everyone, it is easy to make, tastes great and is relatively low in fat and sugar compared to bought varieties. You can also adapt it easily by adding whatever flavours or ingredients you like.

Fresh home-made sorbet. So easy. So fresh. So free from colourings, flavourings and preservatives. And in summer, when there are gluts of fruit, so cheap. What is stopping you adventuring into this world? I encourage you to try whatever fruits you happen to like, or are on special in your market. I've included two classics, which are favourites in our family.

More recently, I have been experimenting with raw ice creams. This has been a revelation. With just a few fresh, raw foods, delicious ice cream can be yours in minutes. Complete guilt-free indulgence. They even pass the kid test.

How to make ice cream

I have a great ice-cream maker, which chills as it churns, but it was a big indulgence. For many years I had a cheap but trusty machine with a bowl that you freeze overnight before making the ice cream. If you have any type of ice-cream maker, just follow the manufacturer's instructions with the recipes in this chapter.

If you don't have an ice-cream maker, do not despair! It is still quite easy to make home-made ice cream.

1. Make the recipe as instructed.

2. Pour the mixture into a robust freezer-proof container and cover.

3. Freeze for a couple of hours.

4. Remove from the freezer and break the ice cream into chunks with a fork.

5. Either mash the mixture well with a fork or pour into a blender or food processor and give it a quick whizz.

6. Repeat steps 2–5 once or twice more. The more times you do it, the smoother it will be, but you'll probably forget and find the ice cream rock solid. Don't worry, just thaw for half an hour or so and whizz or mash again.

Millennium Restaurant

The Artful Vegan, Millennium Restaurant's second cookbook, has always had a special place on my shelf. It's the one I get out when I want to make a pull-all-the-stops-out, impress-all-your-friends (even the really posh non-vegan ones) meal. With lists of ingredients a page long, it's not for the faint-hearted chef, but the instructions are clear and easy to follow and the rewards are worth the extra effort. Recipe titles tantalise with strange and interesting ingredients and combinations; the dish is presented as a gorgeous combination of colours and shapes on the plate and with texture and flavour explosions in your mouth. Just a couple of examples to whet your appetite: black quinoa cake over smoky calypso bean sauce; curried squash and mango-habanero coconut sauce; or white bean-filled filo purse over soft garlic polenta with porcini-zinfandel sauce, broccoli rabe and grilled pear.

The desserts are as beautiful and delicious as the savouries, with a focus on pure and delicate tastes using light and healthy ingredients and local, seasonal fruits (and sometimes even vegetables, for example, apple cake and candy cap flan which includes dried mushrooms). The dishes are low in sugar and fat but high in fascinating flavours.

I knew Millennium had to feature in my book. And when I got the chance to travel through Los Angeles, I decided to give myself a birthday treat and take a side trip to visit the restaurant in San Francisco. We arrived on the day of a special event, the Southern Comfort Annual Dinner, a five-course banquet of food from the American South complete with waiters dressed like farm girls and boys, mint juleps and buckets of beer on the table. The menu sounded like it was going to be heavy, fatty and sugary but of course, being Millennium, they had turned traditional gut-busting, heart-attack-inducing dishes into gourmet vegan cuisine. We had marvellous fun.

It was really hard to decide what to include from Millennium in this book. In the end, I decided to choose something really simple – ice cream. Millennium makes ices and sorbets that are completely yummy, and yet they manage to do it without high fat or high sugar ingredients. I couldn't decide which one I love more, peppermint choc-chunk or peanut butter ice cream, so I included both, and also the raw mango sorbet to show just how simple life can be.

Millennium Restaurant
580 Geary Street
San Francisco
USA
Tel: 415 345 3900

www.millenniumrestaurant.com

Millennium peppermint choc-chunk ice cream   GF

This ice cream is a beautiful green, with a fresh mint flavour – all with no artificial additives or refined sugar. The peppermint blanching is time consuming but quite easy and essential for the lovely colour. This ice cream has been pronounced 'amazing' by my children, high praise indeed.

Makes about 1 litre/2 pints

1½ bars (150 g) chocolate, chopped

1-2 bunches fresh peppermint (or chocolate mint if you grow it, use spearmint if you can't find either)

2½ cups (625 ml) coconut milk

1 cup (250 ml) rice milk

½ cup (125 ml) agave nectar

pinch of salt

1 teaspoon vanilla extract

natural peppermint extract to taste (optional)

Line a large tray with baking parchment.

Melt the chocolate in a bain-marie (see p. 27) and spread melted chocolate thinly over the parchment. Place in freezer until the ice cream is ready.

Fill a medium saucepan with water and add 3 tablespoons salt. Place over a high heat to bring it to a rolling boil. Prepare a bowl or other container with ice water using lots of ice cubes.

Pick all the mint leaves off the stems then drop them all into the boiling water for about 10–15 seconds; the water should make the leaves bright green. Immediately strain the peppermint leaves, and drop them in ice water. This step is necessary as the chlorophyll in the peppermint will oxidise and turn brown if the leaves are not blanched and shocked. Strain cooled peppermint leaves.

Place the strained peppermint and the coconut milk in a blender and blend for about a minute until the coconut milk turns green. Strain the peppermint milk through a cheesecloth or muslin if you have one or a fine sieve if you don't, and return to the blender. Add the remaining ingredients and blend briefly to combine.

Taste and add a few drops of peppermint extract if you feel it needs it.

Freeze by one of the methods on p. 141. When almost frozen, break the chocolate up into the size of chunks you like and fold in.

Millennium mango sorbet   GF LS NF R

Makes about 500 ml/1 pint

3 mangoes, peeled and chopped

¼ cup (60 ml) lime juice

¼ cup (60 ml) orange juice

½ cup (125 ml) water

pinch of salt

1 teaspoon vanilla extract

2-6 tablespoons (30-90 ml) agave nectar

Put all ingredients except agave nectar in a blender or food processor and puree until smooth. Add agave to taste depending on how ripe the mangoes are. Freeze by one of the methods on p. 141.

Millennium peanut butter chocolate chip ice cream GF LS

Put all the ingredients, except the chocolate chips, in the blender or food processor and blend until smooth. Freeze by one of the methods on p. 141, folding in chocolate chips towards the end of the freezing time if desired.

Makes about 1 litre/2 pints

2 cups (500 ml) coconut milk
1½ cups (375 ml) rice milk
½ cup (125 ml) maple syrup or
    agave nectar
1 cup (280 g) peanut butter
    (if salted, omit salt below)
½ teaspoon salt
1½ teaspoons vanilla extract
handful chocolate chips (optional,
    not LS)

vanilla ice cream

Easy-peasy. Don't waste your money on store brands, which are usually expensive and often contain nasties like artificial flavour or colour. If you can, use a good quality, fresh vanilla bean to get the best flavour.

Make a batch of soy custard, omitting the sugar and vanilla – you are going to add these later. Leave to cool, while you whip up a double batch of thin soy cream, again without sweetener or vanilla.

Stir the custard and soy cream together in a large bowl, then mix in the sugar and the vanilla bean seeds. Chill in the fridge for about an hour. Then freeze by one of the methods on p. 141.

Makes 1 litre/2 pints

1 batch (500 ml) soy custard
    (p. 168), without sugar or vanilla
double batch (500 ml) thin
    soy cream (p. 167), without
    sweetener or vanilla
¾ cup (150 g) sugar
seeds of 1 vanilla bean or
    2 teaspoons vanilla extract

brown bread ice cream

I love it when odd ingredients turn up in unexpected places.

Lightly grease a large baking tray.

Blend the bread to fine crumbs in a food processor. Mix with the sugar and spread evenly on the baking tray. Bake for 5 to 7 minutes, until the sugar caramelises and the crumbs are light brown. Cool.

Make a batch of vanilla ice cream. I prefer to reduce the sugar in the ice cream recipe to ½ cup (100 g) instead of ¾ cup (150 g) as the caramelised crumbs are so sweet, but if you have a sweet tooth, just follow the normal recipe.

Freeze by one of the methods on p. 141, stirring in the cooled crumbs before it becomes too firm to stir.

Makes 1 litre/2 pints

1 cup (65 g) brown breadcrumbs
⅓ cup (65 g) brown sugar
1 batch vanilla ice cream (p. 146)

Oven 180°C/350°F/Gas 4

cornet-oh!

My children love being vegan and have pretty healthy eating habits. But they sometimes get sad when they see other kids eating the kind of ice creams you can buy in the shops. So I set about creating a superior version of the chocolate nut cones their friends eat. This divine treat is a bit fiddly, but worth it!

For the cones, break up the chocolate and melt it in a bain-marie (see p. 27). When melted, remove the bowl from the heat and place on a folded tea towel so that it won't slip. Dip each cone deep into the chocolate, rolling the bowl around if you need to, to get a good deep band of chocolate. Hold the cone upside down over the bowl for a few seconds to let it drip. Then pour about a tablespoon of chocolate inside the cone, and again roll it around to coat as much of the inside as you can. Lay the cone on a baking sheet or tray covered with greaseproof paper to cool. Repeat with all the other cones.

To make the praline, place the dairy-free spread and sugar in a small, heavy saucepan and slowly melt. Don't stir as it is melting, just give the pan a shake from time to time. When melted and you can't see any grains of sugar remove from the heat, add the almonds and shake around to coat them all in the caramel. Pour onto a greased baking sheet and bake for 10-15 minutes until the almonds have browned slightly and smell delicious.

Have another baking sheet or tray ready, covered with greaseproof paper. Remove the almonds from the oven, and empty onto the paper-covered tray. When completely cool, place the almonds into a food processor and pulse to a chunky texture. Alternatively, you could put them into a sturdy plastic bag and hit them a few times with a rolling pin until they are the right texture.

For the ice cream, follow directions for the basic vanilla (p. 146). Shortly before the ice cream is frozen, add 4 or 5 tablespoons praline to the mixture. Pour the ice cream into a freezer container, and drizzle 4 or 5 tablespoons fudge sauce over the surface. Use a fork to gently ripple the sauce through the ice cream and freeze.

To serve, scoop ice cream into the cone, top with extra fudge sauce and praline and dive in . . .

Makes 6

CHOCOLATE DIPPED CONES
1 bar (100 g) chocolate
6 waffle cones (or gluten-free
   alternative)

PRALINE
1 tablespoon dairy-free spread
¼ cup (50 g) sugar
¼ cup (35 g) almonds

1 batch vanilla ice cream (p. 146)
1 batch chocolate fudge sauce
   (p. 170)

Oven 180°C/350°F/Gas 4

raspberry sorbet

I first had fresh raspberry sorbet in a wonderful vegetarian B & B in northern France. It was early summer and raspberries were plentiful in the abundant kitchen garden. The sorbet was ruby red and utterly delicious. Every time I make it, I am transported back to that idyllic scene. If only it were always so easy to recapture moments of perfect happiness.

If using frozen raspberries, thaw at room temperature. Put the fresh or thawed raspberries in a blender or food processor with half the syrup and puree. Press the pureed raspberries through a fine-mesh sieve, mix in the lemon juice and remaining syrup, and freeze by one of the methods on p. 141.

Makes about 1 litre/2 pints

4 cups (500 g) fresh or frozen
   raspberries
juice of 1 lemon
2 cups (500 ml) sorbet syrup
   (see box below)

lemon and lime sorbet

Lemon sorbet is my youngest daughter's absolute top dessert. She's always been a sucker for sour and sweet together, and I'm happy to give in to this relatively innocent craving. I've jazzed this one up with lime for an even tarter experience.

Mix the syrup with the rest of the ingredients and freeze by one of the methods on p. 141.

Makes about 750 ml/1½ pints

2 cups (500 ml) sorbet syrup
½ cup (125 ml) lime juice
½ cup (125 ml) lemon juice
finely grated zest of 1 lemon and
   1 lime

Sorbet syrup

4 cups (800 g) sugar

4 cups (1 L) water

Heat the sugar and water in a pan over a moderate heat until the sugar has completely dissolved. Bring to the boil, then remove from the heat and cool. Keep in the fridge until needed.

chocolate chunk ice cream

This is a raw ice cream that delivers a real chocolate punch. I've suggested including the superfoods, lucuma and maca, but these are optional. Lucuma adds a sweet, maple-like flavour and a smooth texture, as well as healthy doses of vitamins A and B, and iron. Maca has a malty, nutty taste and is said to enhance energy and balance the hormone system. You can buy both of these in health food shops.

Blend the brazil nuts and water until smooth. Then strain the mixture through a muslin cloth or nut milk bag, squeezing as much liquid as you can from the mixture.

Put the nut milk and everything else except the chocolate chunks into a blender and puree until very smooth. Freeze by one of the methods on p. 141. Just before the end of the freezing time, add the chocolate chunks and stir in. Serve as it is, or with raw chocolate sauce (p. 170).

Makes about 1 litre/2 pints

1½ cups (225 g) brazil nuts
3 cups (750 ml) water
¼ cup (30 g) raw cacao powder
2 tablespoons soy lecithin, ground
　　to powder in a coffee grinder
2 tablespoons lucuma powder
　　(optional)
2 tablespoons maca powder
　　(optional)
¼ cup (50 g) medjool dates
¼ cup (60 ml) agave nectar
seeds of 1 vanilla bean
pinch of salt
1 batch raw chocolate (p. 187),
　　broken into chunks

strawberry ice cream

GF LS R

This is such a creamy, sweet ice cream that no one will guess it's raw. The banana helps give it a smooth texture, but if you really hate bananas, leave it out.

For the puree, blend the strawberries with the agave nectar. Set aside.

For the ice cream, place the cashews in a blender, add half a cup (125 ml) of water and blend until smooth. Add the remaining water, banana, agave nectar, vanilla seeds, cocoa butter, lecithin and salt. Blend until very smooth. Stir in the strawberry puree and freeze by one of the methods on p. 141. Just before the ice cream is firm, stir in the chopped strawberries.

Makes about 500 ml/1 pint

STRAWBERRY PUREE

2 heaped cups (250 g) strawberries

¼ cup (60 ml) agave nectar

ICE CREAM

1 cup (140 g) cashews, soaked for
   an hour or two

1 cup (250 ml) water

1 small banana

¼ cup (60 ml) agave nectar, or
   to taste

seeds of 1 vanilla bean

1 tablespoon cocoa butter, melted

1 tablespoon soy lecithin, ground
   to a powder in a coffee grinder

pinch of salt

1 cup (125 g) strawberries,
   chopped finely

chapter eight

mousses, custards and creams

There are so many options for replacing dairy in mousses, custards and creams. Soy milk is an easy, creamy option and, if you choose a good brand, the taste is good too. Other 'milks' such as rice or oat milk work well too. You can make your own nut and seed milks quite easily (see p. 8) and these are a nutritious, unadulterated, raw version of the white stuff that we all crave. Other ingredients, like coconut milk and cream, tofu, soaked nuts and even avocado can add a creamy texture to dishes at the same time as supplying valuable nutrients. So you can feel good about indulging in these creamy treats!

Remedy Bliss is one of those radiant, happy people whose very presence convinces you of the benefits of a raw food diet. Remedy set up In the Raw in 2008, running raw food demonstration classes with the aim of creating confidence and giving people the skills they need as they transition to a high raw diet. Remedy's classes are a hoot; her natural humour and vivacity shine through as she takes you on a journey of discovery through the amazing world of raw food. Talking as she creates the food, Remedy shares her extensive knowledge of current food research and enthusiasm for quality, local, organic ingredients and superfoods. The food is incredible: beautiful, fresh, tastebud-tingling. And, when you've eaten, you feel as if your cells are singing with joy, your body thanking you for the gift of pure, natural, life-giving food.

Remedy first encountered the idea of a raw food diet when she met Dr John Fielder, founder of the Academy of Natural Living, in Queensland, Australia, who had been a raw vegan for 40 years. She couldn't believe that someone could exist on raw food alone, however she was immediately convinced on meeting this vibrant, intelligent man; his radiance and amazing clarity reflecting the lifestyle he had chosen. From this meeting, a seed was planted, which a few years later had a chance to fully germinate when Remedy travelled to the USA to take an apprenticeship with Dr Gabriel Cousins at the Tree of Life Rejuvenation Center in Arizona. She spent three months working in the cafe there, learning everything about raw food cuisine and transforming her life. As she says, 'That was it, forever. I knew that was my path.'

For more information about raw food classes, raw film nights and the programme of international speakers on raw issues, please contact Remedy.

Remedy Bliss
In the Raw,
Adelaide
Australia
Tel: 08 8327 1426

remedybliss@gmail.com

In the Raw
chocolate mousse parfait

GF LS R

You will need 4-6 small wine glasses, or dessert dishes.

To make the coconut-cashew cream, put all the ingredients in a food processor or blender and process until quite smooth.

For the chocolate mousse, combine the avocado flesh, agave nectar, vanilla, cacao, cinnamon, salt and ¼ cup of the water in a food processor and blend well. If the mousse seems too thick, add more water, little by little, until it reaches the consistency you prefer.

Fill each glass about a quarter full with coconut-cashew cream, add about half a cup of chopped berries, then top with chocolate mousse. Decorate with berries, a little flaked coconut or a sprig of mint. Refrigerate for half an hour before serving.

How to open a young coconut

1. Place the coconut on its side on a firm cutting board.
2. Use a large, sharp, kitchen knife to cut away the fibrous husk from the top part of the coconut to expose the shell.
3. Stand the coconut up on the chopping board.
4. Use the 'heel' of the knife to hit the coconut shell firmly about a third of the way down to make a hole.
5. Use the heel or the point of the knife to lever the top of the coconut off.
6. Pour out the coconut water and reserve.
7. Use a spatula or spoon to scoop out the white coconut flesh.

Makes 4-6, depending on the size of your dishes

COCONUT-CASHEW CREAM
¼ cup (35 g) cashews (soaked for a few hours or overnight)
2 tablespoons agave nectar
½ cup (80 g) flesh from a young coconut
¼ cup (60 ml) coconut water
2 teaspoons vanilla extract or the seeds of 1 vanilla bean
¼ teaspoon Himalayan salt

CHOCOLATE MOUSSE
2 large avocadoes
½ cup (125 ml) agave nectar
2 teaspoons vanilla extract or the seeds of 1 vanilla bean
1 cup (120 g) raw cacao powder
cinnamon (to taste)
good pinch of Himalayan salt
¼-½ cup (60-125 ml) water

2 punnets berries of your choice

coconut creme brulee

Creme brulee is one of those dairy dishes that I never thought I'd eat again once I became vegan. But crunching your teaspoon through crackly sugar into creamy, custardy depths is an experience that no one should have to sacrifice. So, after many experiments, here is a delicious, crunchy, creamy, cruelty-free brulee. The coconut cream gives a lovely rich texture and hides any possible beany flavour from the tofu. Unrefined coconut palm sugar contributes great flavour and is a healthier and more environmentally friendly alternative to cane sugar, but you can use ordinary sugar if you prefer.

Lightly grease 4-6 small ramekin dishes with oil and place in a baking tin.

Drain the tofu and put it into the food processor with the arrowroot, coconut cream, ¼ cup (50 g) of the sugar, salt and vanilla seeds. Blend well. Divide the mixture between the dishes.

Boil a kettle and pour the water into the bottom of the tin so that it comes about half way up the sides of the ramekins, taking care not to splash water into the custard. Cover just the ramekins with foil – you don't want to seal the foil around the whole pan or it will be too steamy inside. Place the tray into the oven and bake for about 30 minutes or until just set.

Remove the tin from the oven and take the ramekins out of the water bath. Place them in the fridge to cool completely.

There are 3 ways to make the brulee topping:

1. Sprinkle about 1½ teaspoons of sugar on top of each ramekin. Blast them with a mini blowtorch until the sugar caramelises and turns brown and crispy. Chill until quite cold.

2. Preheat your grill to its highest setting. Sprinkle about 1½ teaspoons of sugar on top of each ramekin. Place the dishes under the grill and watch carefully until the sugar caramelises and turns brown and crispy. Remove immediately and chill until quite cold. This method is simple, but it can be hard to caramelise the sugar evenly.

3. Put ¼ cup (50 g) sugar and 2 tablespoons water into a heavy-based pan over a low heat, until the sugar melts. Don't stir the sugar but you can shake the pan every so often to help it melt evenly. Once melted, bring the sugar to a simmer, again without stirring, and let it bubble until it turns a deep caramel colour. This will probably take about 10-15 minutes. When the whole thing is brown and bubbling, remove from the heat and carefully pour about a tablespoon on top of each ramekin. Roll the dish around to cover the top evenly, and chill until quite cold.

Makes 4-6

1¼ cups (300 g) soft silken tofu

2 tablespoons arrowroot

½ cup (125 ml) coconut cream

½ cup (100 g) coconut palm sugar (see p. 10)

pinch of salt

seeds of 1 vanilla bean

Oven 170°C/325°F/Gas 3

perfect chocolate mousse

GF NF

This is so simple but so good. It all depends on the quality of the chocolate, so don't stint here. Go for a brand with 70% cocoa solids. You could also experiment with flavoured chocolate. It works well with orange or peppermint. I like to serve this mousse in tiny espresso coffee cups.

You will need 8 small cups or glasses.

Melt the chocolate in a bain-marie (see p. 27). Remove chocolate from the heat and cool a little until it becomes slightly thicker. Don't omit this step because if you add hot chocolate to cold cream the chocolate will seize and you'll have a lumpy, hard mixture (if this does happen to you, don't despair, just let it cool, then roll into truffles – it still tastes good!). Whip the cream with a balloon whisk in a large bowl until it is full of tiny bubbles (it won't thicken much). Add melted chocolate little by little to the soy cream, whisking as you go. Then stir in 2 tablespoons sugar syrup and the vanilla extract. Taste to see if sweet enough and correct by adding more sugar syrup if necessary.

Spoon the mousse into small cups or glasses, and place in the refrigerator to set.

Makes 8

2 bars (200 g) good quality dark
  chocolate
1½ cups (375 ml) thin soy cream
  (p. 167)
¼ cup (60 ml) sorbet syrup (p. 150)
½ teaspoon vanilla extract

zen green tea coconut custard

I am grateful to Stephen Galpin, an inspirational Ayurvedic chef (www.ayurvedickitchen.com.au), for passing on this recipe to me and allowing me to adapt and share it. It contains home-made coconut milk, coconut oil, green tea, kuzu and jaggery – all ingredients which have myriad health benefits – and happens to be utterly delicious too.

You will need 4 ramekin dishes.

To make the coconut milk, place the coconut in a blender, add the water and blend vigorously for a couple of minutes. Let it stand for 30 minutes. Strain the mixture through a muslin cloth or very fine sieve, squeezing out as much liquid as you can. You can use the leftover coconut pulp for cakes and biscuits.

For the custard, dissolve the green tea in a little warm water and set aside. Pound the kuzu to a powder in a mortar and pestle.

In a large saucepan, mix the kuzu powder to a paste with a little cold water. Add the coconut milk, coconut oil and jaggery and mix well until all the ingredients are blended.

Cook on a medium heat, whisking all the time, until the mixture starts to thicken. This should take about 5 minutes. As soon as it thickens, remove from the heat and whisk well to get rid of any lumps. Reduce the heat, return the pan to the stove and simmer for 3 to 4 minutes, whisking all the time until the mixture becomes smooth and glossy. Remove from the heat and stir in the green tea paste.

Pour the custard into the ramekins while still hot. Eat warm, or cool to room temperature when the custards can be turned out and served on a small plate.

Makes 4

COCONUT MILK

2½ cups (250 g) desiccated
    coconut, or fresh coconut flesh
2½ cups (625 ml) water, boiled
    in a kettle and allowed to cool
    slightly

CUSTARD

1 teaspoon powdered green tea
½ cup (60 g) kuzu (p. 14)
2½ cups (625 ml) coconut milk
2 tablespoons coconut oil
2 tablespoons (25 g) jaggery
    (p. 10), crumbled

cream

What, you've been paying good money for soy cream? Can you believe this is so easy to make? And, of course, it's much healthier than the dairy version because it uses unrefined sweeteners and unsaturated fat. Ideally, you should use a stick blender for this cream, if you have one. If you're using an upright blender or food processor, you may find it hard to get the cream to thicken. Some soy milks work better than others for this recipe so, if you're having trouble getting it to thicken, try a different brand.

Mix the maple syrup or agave nectar and vanilla with the soy milk in a tall, narrow container that your stick blender will fit into. Put the blender in right to the bottom and switch it on. Keep the blender running, hold your container still and slowly drizzle in the oil. This can feel like it takes 3 hands, and if you have a friend around by all means rope them in. But, with practice, you'll get the hang of it. As you add the oil, the cream will start to thicken. If you're making the thick cream you may think it is never going to thicken enough; then suddenly, with just a few more drops of oil, it will.

Makes 1 cup

THICK CREAM

⅓ cup (80 ml) soy milk – it's got to be soy; rice or oat just won't thicken

⅔ cup (160 ml) light oil, e.g. sunflower

1 tablespoon maple syrup or agave nectar

½ teaspoon vanilla extract

THIN CREAM

½ cup (125 ml) soy milk

½ cup (125 ml) oil

1 tablespoon maple syrup or agave nectar

½ teaspoon vanilla extract

cashew cream

Put the cashews, agave nectar, water, vanilla seeds and salt in a blender and blend until very smooth. Leave the motor running as you add the coconut oil. Chill.

Makes about 1 cup

1 cup (140 g) cashews, soaked for an hour or two

2 tablespoons agave nectar

½ cup (125 ml) water

seeds of 1 vanilla bean

pinch of salt

1 tablespoon coconut oil, melted

custard

I know there are some people who make their custard using eggs and milk, but let's be honest, most people just mix up custard powder, sugar and milk. Most custard powder is vegan, so you could just make it up with any non-dairy milk you like. Or you could make this cheaper version, which includes all the ingredients in custard powder, except the yellow food colouring, which I have replaced with turmeric.

Mix the cornflour, sugar, vanilla and turmeric to a paste with a little of the milk in a large jug or bowl. Warm the rest of the milk in a non-stick pan over a moderate heat until it is steaming but not boiling. Pour the warm milk into the cornflour-sugar paste, whisking as you go, then pour the whole lot back into the pan and let it come to the boil, stirring all the time. Turn the heat to low and continue to stir as you simmer the custard for about 2 minutes to thicken it and cook the cornflour. Be careful, as custard easily sticks and burns.

Makes 500 ml/1 pint

2-3 tablespoons cornflour, depending on how thick you like it

1-2 tablespoons sugar

1 teaspoon vanilla extract or the seeds of 1 vanilla bean

pinch of turmeric

2 cups (500 ml) non-dairy milk

chocolate ganache

This is my all-time favourite sweet thing to eat as a topping for ice cream or drizzled over cupcakes, brownies, cookies or flapjacks. If you let it cool in the fridge, ganache can be shaped into balls and rolled in cocoa for easy truffles. Certain members of my family are guilty of dipping spoons, or even fingers, into the bowl whenever they peer in the fridge looking for inspiration.

Melt chocolate in a bain-marie (see p. 27). Let it cool slightly while you measure the other ingredients into a small food processor bowl or hand blender jug. Then add the chocolate and whizz for about a minute, until the ganache becomes thick and glossy.

If frosting a large cake, pour over the cake immediately allowing it to dribble over the sides in thick, oozing runnels. Or drizzle with a spoon over small cakes or bars. If storing in the fridge, pour the ganache into the bowl you used for melting the chocolate. To re-melt it, simply put the bowl over a pan of simmering water again.

Makes about 2 cups

2 bars (200 g) chocolate, chopped
⅔ cup (160 ml) soy milk
2 tablespoons maple syrup
1 teaspoon vanilla extract

chocolate fudge sauce

An essential ingredient in the Cornet-oh! (p. 149) and great on all kinds of desserts, this is low in fat and lower in sugar than many similar sauces.

Mix the sugar, cocoa and arrowroot in a jug or bowl, and mix to a paste with a little of the milk. Heat the rest of the milk in a non-stick saucepan. When it is steaming but not boiling, pour over the sugar-cocoa paste, whisking all the time. Return to the pan and heat gently, stirring all the time, until it thickens. Add the vanilla and salt and stir well.

Makes about 2 cups

½ cup (100 g) sugar
¼ cup (30 g) cocoa
2 teaspoons arrowroot
1 cup (250 ml) soy or rice milk
1 teaspoon vanilla extract
pinch of salt

easy chocolate sauce

Similar to ganache, but quicker. This is great for a last-minute ice cream sauce.

Warm the soy milk gently. When it is steaming but not boiling, remove from the heat and stir in the chocolate. Add the maple syrup or agave and stir until melted.

Makes about ¾ cup

¼ cup (60 ml) soy milk
½ cup (75 g) chocolate, chopped
1 tablespoon maple syrup or
   agave nectar

raw chocolate sauce

Great as a topping for ice cream and cakes – or add to warmed almond milk for a delicious chocolate drink. Don't even save it for the raw stuff, everyone loves this easy sauce.

Mix the cacao, cinnamon and salt. Stir the syrup into the cacao mixture little by little until it forms a smooth paste. Add the vanilla. Add water until it is the texture you require. This keeps for ages in the fridge.

Makes ¼ cup

¼ cup (30 g) raw cacao
tiny pinch of cinnamon
tiny pinch of salt
2 tablespoons maple syrup or
   agave nectar
½ teaspoon vanilla extract
1-3 tablespoons water

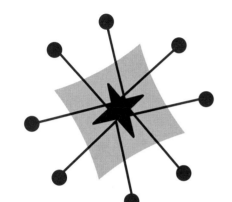

chapter nine

sweet bites

It is the sad truth that this is where vegans really miss out. Which could be a good or a bad thing, depending on how you look at it. On the one hand, we can never grab a chocolate bar when we stand in line at the petrol station or supermarket checkout. On the other hand, we are not tempted to grab a chocolate bar *every* time we stand in line at the petrol station or supermarket checkout and thus we avoid excessive consumption of saturated fats, refined sugar and artificial additives.

And when we do make the effort to produce our own sweets they are full of quality ingredients and taste all the better for it. Here is a lovely selection of healthy and not-so-healthy tasty morsels for special occasions, parties, or just because.

When I first moved to Adelaide I searched the internet for vegan places to eat and somewhere to practice yoga. I knew there was some magic going on when I found Bliss, an organic, vegan cafe, with the Centre Om yoga studio upstairs! My family and I visited Bliss lots of times over the next few months, enjoying its beautiful courtyard garden, healthy food and laid-back atmosphere. We liked it so much that, when we heard through the grapevine that the owners were thinking of leaving, we offered to buy the cafe. We ran Bliss for just over a year and had a wonderful time meeting lovely people, inventing, creating and experimenting with vegan food, and learning rapidly about the pleasures and pitfalls of running a small business in Australia. When we passed on the reins to the new owners, it was with a mixture of sadness and relief. It was great to feel that we didn't have to neglect our two (home-schooled) children anymore, and that we could have the occasional day off, but I will always have a soft spot in my heart for lovely Bliss.

The new owners, Kas and Shane, demonstrate the same passion and commitment to the cafe, continuing to provide homemade vegan food that is also local, organic and fairtrade whenever possible. On the menu are delicious breakfasts, home-made burgers, curries, soups, salads and cakes; organic, fairtrade coffee and tea; delicious hot chocolate and chai; and a variety of freshly squeezed juices and smoothies. There are many raw options, too. The cafe is a venue for movie screenings, live music nights and monthly art exhibitions. It's also a great place to stock up on all your vegan needs, from cookbooks to vegan cheese to chocolate.

Bliss Organic Cafe
7 Compton St
Adelaide
Australia
Tel: 08 8231 0205

www.blissorganiccafe.com.au

Bliss Organic Cafe

Garden Courtyard
*
FREE Wi-Fi
*
Gluten-free
options
*
Live Music
*
Children's
Corner
*
RAW dishes
*
COMING UP:
Feb-March
Tiny Towns
*
A Sure Cat
Ciao Ta
5 Feb 6pm
Wandering
Minstrels
12 Feb 6pm
Live Music
19 Feb 1pm
Georgia
Germein
21 Feb 1pm
Tears of
Candle
24 Feb 6pm
David Hope
FREE ENTRY
Book Signing
26 Feb 8pm
Black Ruby

Bliss
Organic
& garden café

Live music
this Friday

Bliss Organic Cafe bliss balls

GF LS R

Bliss balls are a raw, not too sweet, satisfying treat. They are easy and quick to make and contain so many excellent ingredients that they could be considered a superfood in a ball.

Grind the almonds just a little in a food processor, add the dates and blend a bit more, then add the prunes and blend again. It's important to add the ingredients in this order to get the right consistency. Once the fruits are chopped quite well, add the walnuts, seeds and coconut and whizz a bit more. Add the carob powder at the end. The mixture should be dark, sticky and easy to work with.

Put 2-3 tablespoons of coconut into a small bowl. Using your hands, roll the bliss ball mixture into balls the size of a golf ball and roll in the shredded coconut to coat.

Bliss balls keep well for up to a week.

Makes about 24

1 cup (140 g) almonds

2 cups (320 g) dates, pitted and chopped

2 cups (320 g) prunes, pitted and chopped

1 cup (100 g) walnuts

½ cup (75 g) sunflower seeds

½ cup (75 g) pumpkin seeds

¼ cup (35 g) sesame seeds

¼ cup (25 g) shredded or desiccated coconut

¼ cup (30 g) carob powder, or raw cacao, or a mixture of the two

2-3 tablespoons shredded or desiccated coconut, for coating

ALTERNATIVES

- cashew nuts or hazelnuts (instead of walnuts or use a mixture of the two)
- try coating with cacao powder, carob powder, crushed nuts, poppy seeds or sesame seeds instead of coconut

liqueur truffles

These make lovely presents, if you can bear to give them away.

Melt the chocolate and dairy-free spread together in a bain-marie (see p. 27). Scrape the vanilla seeds from the pod, and add the seeds and the empty pod to the milk. Warm the milk in a small pan over a gentle heat for about 2 minutes to allow the flavours of the vanilla to infuse. Do not let the milk boil. Remove from the heat and allow to cool a little.

When the chocolate has melted, remove the bowl from the heat and allow to cool a little. Remove the empty vanilla pod from the milk and stir in the liqueur, if using. Add the milk to the chocolate. Stir well until everything is blended. Pour the chocolate mixture into a large glass or ceramic dish and chill until set.

Sift the cocoa onto a plate. Use a teaspoon to scrape curls out of the truffle mixture. Press the curls gently into a ball shape, but avoid pressing them together too tightly. Roll each truffle gently in the cocoa to coat. Store in the fridge.

Makes about 24

3½ bars (350 g) chocolate

2 tablespoons (25 g) dairy-free spread

seeds of 1 vanilla bean

½ cup (125 ml) soy milk

2 tablespoons brandy or other liqueur (optional)

2 tablespoons cocoa

christmas apricots and dates

GF LS R

These lovely little Middle Eastern sweets look pretty on a platter and satisfy the sweetest tooth.

To make the apricots, soak the almonds in boiling water for a couple of minutes. Remove from the water and slip off their skins. Place on a baking tray and roast for 7–10 minutes until lightly browned. Leave to cool. If you prefer to keep the recipe raw, just use raw, unskinned almonds. Chop 12 of the almonds coarsely and mix with the chopped prunes, cinnamon and maple syrup. In a separate bowl, mix the chopped pistachios and sesame seeds. Cut a slit down the side of each apricot, use your fingers to create a pocket, and stuff a spoonful of prune mixture inside. Roll in the pistachio/sesame seed mixture and poke a whole almond into the top.

For the dates, carefully slit each date across one side and remove the stone. Spoon in half a teaspoon of tahini and place a brazil nut inside each date. Close the date and arrange on a plate. If desired, melt the chocolate in a bain-marie (see p. 27) and drizzle over the dates. Leave to set.

Makes 12 of each

APRICOTS

24 whole almonds

⅓ cup (50 g) ready-to-eat prunes, finely chopped

1 teaspoon ground cinnamon

2 tablespoons maple syrup

¼ cup (30 g) pistachios, finely chopped

1 tablespoon sesame seeds

12 ready-to-eat dried apricots

DATES

12 medjool dates

2 tablespoons tahini

12 large brazil nuts

¼ bar (25 g) chocolate (optional, omit for LS or R)

Oven 170°C/325°F/Gas 3

panforte

There are lots of stories about the origins of panforte, but the one I like the best is this one. A nun in 13th century Siena, finding that mice had eaten through all the sacks in the pantry and that there was a huge pile of nuts, dried fruits, sugar and spices all mixed together, decided to make it all into a cake rather than throwing it away. And so panforte was born. Aside from the health and safety angle, I guess this appeals to my minimal waste mentality; I just love making something yummy from what's left in the store cupboard. Before you get agitated about my suggestion to use honey, read what I have to say about it on p. 11. And use agave or maple syrup if you prefer. Panforte keeps well for several weeks, wrapped in baking parchment.

Grease and line with baking parchment a 23 cm (9") round cake tin.

Soak the sultanas or raisins in the brandy or orange juice for about an hour. Leave half the almonds whole and chop the other half and the hazelnuts coarsely.

Put the nuts, ground almonds, mixed peel, spices and lemon zest in a large bowl and mix well. Add the soaked sultanas or raisins.

Heat the sugar and honey, agave nectar or maple syrup gently until the sugar melts, then heat until the mixture bubbles madly. Keep at this heat for 2 minutes (if you have a sugar thermometer, until the mixture reaches 115°C). Remove from the heat and pour into the nut and fruit mixture. Working quickly, mix well and spread the mixture into the cake tin, dipping your spoon into a jug of hot water occasionally so you can smooth it flat.

Bake for 30 minutes, then cool in the tin on a wire rack. Turn out when cool. Sprinkle with icing sugar to serve.

Serves 10-12

¾ cup (120 g) sultanas or raisins
1 tablespoon brandy or
    orange juice
¾ cup (100 g) almonds, skinned
    and toasted (see p. 15)
¾ cup (100 g) hazelnuts, toasted
    and skinned (see p. 15)
½ cup (70 g) ground almonds
1¼ cups (170 g) chopped
    mixed peel
1 teaspoon cinnamon
¼ teaspoon mixed spice
2 cloves, ground
1 teaspoon lemon zest
⅔ cup (130 g) brown sugar, firmly
    packed
½ cup (125 ml) honey, agave nectar
    or maple syrup

Oven 150°C/300°F/Gas 2

rice crispy crackles

GF

This recipe is a real English/Australian hybrid. What it gets from its English parent is real chocolate, and golden syrup to make it gooey. The Australian parent has passed on desiccated coconut and cocoa. The white, hydrogenated fat usually included in the Aussie version has evolved into much healthier dairy-free spread, and sultanas add an extra chewy dimension.

Line a muffin tin with paper liners.

Melt the chocolate in a bain-marie (see p. 27). In a large pan, melt the dairy-free spread, then add the syrup. When melted, add the cocoa and a pinch of salt and stir well. Remove from the heat, then stir the chocolate into the pan. Mix in the rest of the ingredients and stir well to coat. Fill the paper liners and leave to set in the fridge.

Serves 12

1 bar (100 g) chocolate, chopped
½ cup (100 g) dairy-free spread
¼ cup (60 ml) golden syrup
¼ cup (30 g) cocoa
pinch of salt
3 cups (100 g) puffed rice cereal
½ cup (50 g) desiccated coconut
½ cup (75 g) sultanas

chocolate crunch

When I first created this recipe, it became such a favourite in our family that people would choose it for their birthday cake, and I think we had it for Christmas dessert a few years running too.

Grease a 20 cm x 30 cm (8" x 12") rectangular tin.

Melt the dairy-free spread and golden syrup. Remove from the heat. Add the cocoa and stir until dissolved. Add the biscuit crumbs, dried fruit and chopped nuts and stir well. Press into the tin, level off and chill until firm.

Melt the chocolate in a bain-marie (see p. 27), then pour over the base and roll the pan around to coat the surface evenly. Chill until set, then mark into small squares.

Serves 10-12

½ cup (100 g) dairy-free spread
½ cup (200 g) golden syrup
¾ cup (100 g) cocoa
1 cup (100 g) digestive biscuits, broken into crumbs
⅔ cup (100 g) raisins or sultanas
½ cup (50 g) pecans or walnuts, chopped
1½ bars (150 g) chocolate

carob clusters

Chewy, sticky, nutty treats that are full of goodness.

Line a baking tray with parchment paper.

Melt the peanut butter, maple syrup or agave nectar, tahini and salt in a large pan over a low heat. Stir in the rest of the ingredients.

Use your hands to form clusters the size of a golf ball. Place on the baking tray and chill.

Makes 12-14

½ cup (150 g) peanut or
   almond butter

⅓ cup (80 ml) maple syrup or
   agave nectar

2 tablespoons tahini

pinch of salt

⅓ cup (40 g) carob powder

½ cup (50 g) walnuts or almonds,
   chopped

¼ cup (35 g) pumpkin seeds

¼ cup (35 g) sesame seeds

¼ cup (35 g) sunflower seeds

¼ cup (25 g) desiccated coconut

¼ cup (40 g) sultanas or
   chopped dates

raw chocolate

GF LS R

Raw chocolate has an intense, rich flavour and is really easy to make. Fill any size mould for chocolate pure and simple. Spread thinly on baking parchment and break it up to use as chocolate chunks in raw ice cream (p. 153) or as a decoration for black forest gateau (p. 40). For a yummy nut cup, layer chocolate with almond fudge (p. 62) in miniature cake cases. Try flavouring with natural peppermint or orange extract, liqueurs, chopped nuts or dried fruits.

Melt the cacao butter in a glass bowl in a dehydrator, or set over another bowl of hot water. When it is melted, stir in the agave nectar, then add the cacao powder and mix well.

If the mixture starts to stiffen up, don't panic. This can happen but, unlike ordinary chocolate, raw chocolate can be rescued. Simply put the bowl back in the dehydrator or over a bowl of hot water for a few minutes, then whisk until it becomes smooth and glossy again.

Pour into chosen moulds and put in the freezer to set. Store in the fridge or freezer.

⅓ cup (40 g) cacao butter
2 tablespoons agave nectar
⅓ cup (40 g) raw cacao powder

food allergy index

Everything in this book is free from animal ingredients: eggs, dairy, gelatine – or other animal additives.

In addition, many of the recipes are suitable for people following gluten-free, wheat-free, raw, low sugar and nut-free diets. Look for the code on each recipe, and here is a complete list for easy reference.

Do be careful when using processed ingredients, for example, soy milk, baking powder, icing sugar and cornflour. Many products contain added sugars and gluten-containing ingredients, and cannot guarantee that they are nut free. Check the labelling carefully and, if you are in any doubt, contact the manufacturer for more information.

gluten free GF

Chocolate ganache 168
Chocolate sauces: fudge, easy, raw 170
Chocolate torte 36
Christmas apricots and dates 179
Christmas pudding (with gluten-free flour and breadcrumbs) 123
Cinnamon apple raisin muffins 54
Coconut creme brulee 160
Coconut rice pudding 111
Cornet-oh! 149
Custard 168
De Bolhoed Dutch apple pie (with gluten-free pastry) 73
Double fudge pecan brownies 50
Eccles cakes (with gluten-free pastry) 86
Fruit mince pies (with gluten-free pastry) 77
Gluten-free vanilla cake 45
Hungarian cheese pie (with gluten-free pastry) 78
In the Raw chocolate mousse parfait 159
Lancrigg fig and almond pudding 106
le cru pineapple carpaccio 126
Lemon and lime sorbet 150
Lemon raspberry trifle (with gluten-free sponge) 100
Lime tart 95
Liqueur truffles 176
Mango sorbet 144
Millennium peppermint choc-chunk ice cream 144
Mini peach pies 85
Panforte 180
Perfect chocolate mousse 163
Raspberry sorbet 150
Raw chocolate 187
Revel chocolate midnight cake 91
Rice crispy crackles 183
Strawberry ice cream 154
Summer pudding (with gluten-free bread) 137
Tarte tatin (with gluten-free pastry) 81
Tiramisu (with gluten-free sponge) 99
Vanilla ice cream 146
Vanilla-poached pears with hazelnut-fig filling 130
Vitality cake 39
Walnut treacle tart (with gluten-free pastry and breadcrumbs) 74
Winter fruit compote 127
Zen green tea coconut custard 164

wheat free

EVERYTHING LISTED UNDER GLUTEN FREE, PLUS:
Anzac biscuits 57
Bags of energy bars 65
Chocoblock cookies 64
Plum and pecan crumble 112
Real Food Daily double chocolate layer cake with
    raspberry puree 27
Steve's flapjacks 53
Wheat-free vanilla cake 44

low sugar

(less than 12g/serving, see p. 9)

Almond and lemon cantucci 58
Amaretto peacherines 129
Anzac biscuits 57
Apple and strawberry jelly 133
Baked apples 138
Bags of energy bars 65
Black forest gateau 40
Bliss Organic Cafe bliss balls 175
Bread and butter pudding 119
Carob clusters 185
Cashew cream 167
Chocoblock cookies 64
Chocolate chunk ice cream 153
Chocolate mousse parfait 159
Christmas apricots and dates 179
Christmas pudding 123
Cinnamon apple raisin muffins 54
Coconut rice pudding 111
Cream 167
Custard 168
De Bolhoed Dutch apple pie 73
Devon scones with jam and cream 61
Eccles cakes 86
Fruit mince pies 77
Five-grain pancakes with flambeed bananas 134
Lancrigg fig and almond pudding 106
Lime tart 95

Mango sorbet 144
Mini peach pies 85
Peanut butter ice cream 145
Plum and pecan crumble 112
Raw chocolate 187
Spiced carrot cake 31
Steve's flapjacks 53
Strawberry ice cream 154
Vanilla-poached pears with hazelnut-fig filling 130
Vitality cake 39
Winter fruit compote 127
Zen green tea coconut custard 164

nut free NF

Anzac biscuits 57
Apple and blackberry betty 115
Baked apples 138
Banoffi tarts 103
Berry cobbler 116
Bread and butter pudding 119
Bread pudding 110
Brown bread ice cream 147
Chocolate ganache 168
Chocolate sauces: fudge, easy, raw 170
Chocolate torte 36
Christmas pudding 123
Coconut creme brulee 160
Cream 167
Custard 168
Double fudge brownies (omit pecans) 50
Eccles cakes 86
Five grain pancakes with flambeed bananas 134
Hello daddy chocolate berry pie 96
Hungarian cheese pie 78
Lemon and lime sorbet 150

Lemon raspberry trifle (omit almonds) 100
Lemon syrup sponge pudding 120
Liqueur truffles (omit nut-based liqueur) 176
Mango sorbet 144
Matrimonial cake 67
Mini peach pies (omit Amaretto and almond extract) 85
New York-style lemon cheesecake 92
Perfect chocolate mousse 163
le cru pineapple carpaccio 126
Raspberry sorbet 150
Real Food Daily double chocolate layer cake with
    raspberry puree 27
Sticky date pudding 109
Summer pudding 137
Tarte tatin 81
Three kinds of vanilla cake 43-45
Tiramisu (omit Amaretto) 99
Vanilla ice cream 146
Winter fruit compote 127

raw R

Bags of energy bars 65
Black forest gateau 40
Bliss Organic Cafe bliss balls 175
Cashew cream 167
Chocolate chunk ice cream 153
Chocolate mousse parfait 159
Christmas apricots and dates 179
le cru pineapple carpaccio 126
Lime tart 95
Mango sorbet 144
Raw chocolate 187
Raw chocolate sauce 170
Strawberry ice cream 154
Winter fruit compote 127

index

conversion tables

All conversions are approximate, for ease of use.

Liquid measurement

Volume	UK/Europe	USA/Canada
1 teaspoon	5 ml	⅛ fl. oz (5 ml)
1 tablespoon	20 ml (15 ml UK/Europe)	½ fl. oz (15 ml)
¼ cup	60 ml	2 fl. oz
⅓ cup	80 ml	2.5 fl. oz
½ cup	125 ml	4 fl. oz
⅔ cup	160 ml	5 fl. oz
¾ cup	180 ml	6 fl. oz
1 cup	250 ml	8 fl. oz
1 pint	575 ml (20 fl. oz)	16 fl. oz (475 ml)
1 quart	—	32 fl. oz (950 ml)

Oven temperatures

° Celsius	° Fahrenheit	Gas	Temperature
120	250	¼	very cool
140	275	1	cool
150	300	2	cool
170	325	3	warm
180	350	4	moderate
190	375	5	fairly hot
200	400	6	hot
220	425	7	very hot
230	450	8	very hot

Weight

Metric	Imperial
15 g	½ ounce
30 g	1 ounce
100 g	3.5 ounces
115 g	4 ounces
225 g	8 ounces
450 g	1 pound

Other vegan books published by Grub Street

Vegan with a Vengeance
Over 150 delicious, cheap animal-free recipes
Isa Chandra Moskowitz
978-1-904943-66-2

How It All Vegan!
Irresistible recipes for an animal-free diet
Tanya Barnard and Sarah Kramer
978-1-906502-07-2

Eat Smart Eat Raw
Kate Wood
978-1-904010-12-8

Raw Living
Kate Wood
978-1-904943-74-7

For a complete full colour catalogue of all our cookbooks
email food@grubstreet.co.uk
or visit our website
www.grubstreet.co.uk
And follow us on Twitter @grub_street